BONHOEFFER

The Man and his Work

BONHOEFFER

The Man and his Work

RENÉ MARLÉ

Translated by
ROSEMARY SHEED

NEWMAN PRESS
New York, N.Y. Glen Rock, N.J.
Amsterdam Toronto London

A Newman Press edition, originally published under the title *Dietrich Bonhoeffer, Témoin de Jésus-Christ parmi ses frères* by Casterman, Tournai, © 1967.

Published by Newman Press
Editorial Office: 304 W. 58th St., N.Y., N.Y. 10019
Business Office: Glen Rock, N.J. 07452

Library of Congress Catalog Card Number: 68-8395

Printed and bound in Great Britain

Contents

Acknowledgements

The Publisher gratefully acknowledges the permission of Harper and Row, Inc., New York and The Macmillan Co., New York to quote from the following translations of Bonhoeffer's writing:

Harper and Row Inc: *Life Together*, 1954; *No Rusty Swords*, 1965; *The Way to Freedom*, 1966.
The Macmillan Co: *Ethics* (page references are to the Fontana edition), 1955; *The Cost of Discipleship*, 1959; *Letters and Papers from Prison*, revised and enlarged edition, 1967.

Foreword

THE name of Bonhoeffer is now among those most often referred to in religious discussions. There are many people almost everywhere ready to make him into a latter day prophet.

Yet their basis for doing so is often slight enough. Many of Bonhoeffer's admirers, indeed, know him only through Robinson's *Honest to God*; and Robinson himself makes use only of the letters from prison. Furthermore, he mixes up Bonhoeffer's ideas with those of Bultmann and Tillich, whose theology is very differently inspired.

Even those who have actually read some of Bonhoeffer's writings, especially *Letters and Papers from Prison*, in general still have only a somewhat fragmentary knowledge of the man and his work. It is all too likely, then, that the true significance and scope of the bold themes in his last reflexions from prison—which have with good reason awoken so many echoes in recent years—will be only imperfectly grasped.

At the time of working them out, Bonhoeffer himself was aware both of their inchoate and indefinite nature, and of the continuity he could always recognize in his life and thinking throughout all the obvious developments they were subjected to. And his friend Bethge, to whom most of the letters from prison were addressed, and who has edited the larger part of his work, also stresses the organic unity among the different stages of his correspondent's career.

It may come as a surprise to those who only know Bonhoeffer through Robinson, to learn that when I myself first (over ten years ago now) got to know him, through the letters from prison, he appeared to me in the guise of a valuable antidote within Protestantism itself to the impoverishing influence of Bultmann, whose theses I was setting out to analyse at the time. His reflexion on the 'penultimate things' which are not to be singly argued away, on the decisive importance of the Old Testament in preventing the Christian faith from developing into a disembodied idealism, his sense of the worth of 'natural' things: all this seemed to me just what was needed to set right, by going to the very heart of the matter, the narrow concept developed by Bultmann, of a purely 'eschatological' faith, a faith, that is exercized only upon the extremities of the world and history and passing over all the realities of experience and life. And when, some years later, I was asked by a colleague whether I had heard of Bonhoeffer, who was said to be more 'frightening' than Bultmann, and to go 'much further' in watering down the Christian faith, I could hardly contain my astonishment, and indeed indignation, at what seemed to me so serious a misconception.

The conviction I got, from the first, of Bonhoeffer as someone rich and complex, with ideas that could never be expressed in a few slogans, became continually stronger as I came to know all his other published work.

It is this knowledge, which has ripened over the years, that I want to try to pass on here. Having sketched out a portrait of the man, and his short life, I want to pick out the key ideas developed in his works, and the basic intuitions upon which his behaviour rested. Thus we will look in turn at his major works. But Bonhoeffer's thought does not unfold according to a purely logical system. Some themes suggested in early writings only develop in depth in the later ones; others upon which he lays great stress early on are only taken up *en passant* later on; still others appear only occasionally, in letters, sermons, or lectures. That is why, though I am centering the various sections of this book upon the major works in their order of publication, I will often introduce elements that really belong to other writings, but which, since they flow from the same inspiration, are useful in casting light on the ideas being developed in those under consideration. This book will thus quite naturally reflect in its own structure that diversity in unity, that development in continuity, which Bonhoeffer himself was conscious of in his life and thought, and which seems to me such an important characteristic of the message he has left us.

I

Unusual Man—Unusual Destiny

Thought and life are inseparable in Bonhoeffer. Both, moreover, are linked with the agonized history of Germany and the world in the years between 1925 and 1945. His work, the work of an outstanding mind, is also the expression of his character. That is why, before approaching a theology which, though not shirking technicality, was always seen by its author in terms of action and service, and before trying to interpret a message which was never completely expressed, it is important to get to know the man, and to see him in the context of the extraordinary circumstances he was faced with.

An aristocrat

That Bonhoeffer was an aristocrat means that we must look first at his family. His father was a great doctor, a psychiatrist and neurologist. His mother, Paula von Hase, was the daughter of a chaplain at the Emperor's court, and the grand-daughter of a famous ecclesiastical historian, Karl von Hase. Into this upper middle class German world he was born, in Breslau, on 4 February 1906.

In 1912 he followed his family to Berlin, where his father had been appointed professor of psychiatry at the university. The Bonhoeffers then lived with their eight children in the smart district of Grünewald. The most distinguished exponents of German culture, professors at the university of the imperial capital, generally lived in the luxurious villas of Grünewald. Adolf von Harnack was a close neighbour and great friend of the Bonhoeffer family. Very early on, the young Dietrich was brought to the musical evenings so dear to the German middle class, and soon he would be old enough to join in the conversations at which the intellectual elite of a Berlin then at the summit of its prestige enjoyed meeting together.

However, it is not so much his social origin that makes Bonhoeffer appear to us as an aristocrat, as his own character. An American friend Paul Lehmann remembers him best as the representative of 'an aristocracy of the mind, in the best sense of the word'.[1] And his twin sister Sabine describes him as a 'chivalrous young man'.[2]

In May 1945 there was found, hidden between the tiles of a roof, a twenty-page manuscript which Bonhoeffer had written for some of his friends in the resistance, which was an attempt to express the experience of the kind of night-fighting they used to do, and the values they were setting out to defend. One of the most important paragraphs deals with the 'sense of quality'. This indicates one of the key traits in Bonhoeffer's spirit.

> Unless we have the courage to fight for a revival of wholesome reserve between man and man, we shall perish in an anarchy of human values. . . . When we forget what is due to ourselves and to others, when the feeling for human quality and the power to exercise reserve cease to exist, chaos is at the door.[3]

As always, Bonhoeffer is quite conscious of speaking within an existing situation. He felt a deep distaste for a régime in which mediocrity could triumph unopposed, and in which vulgarity was lurking visibly beneath the tinsel of pseudo-virtues.

> In other times it may have been the business of Christianity to champion the equality of all men; its business today will be to defend passionately human dignity and reserve.[4]

This 'difference', to which Bonhoeffer returns several times, involves no element of contempt. Indeed it was contempt that lay at the bottom of the whole Nazi ideology against which Bonhoeffer and his friends stood so firmly. It seemed to him one of the most serious temptations and evils.

[1] *Begegnung mit Bonhoeffer. Ein Almanach*, Munich, 1964, 38.
[2] *Ibid.*, 21. [3] *Letters and Papers from Prison*, 35.
[4] *Ibid.*

> There is a very real danger of our drifting into an attitude of contempt for humanity. . . . It means that we at once fall into the worst blunders of our opponents. . . . The only profitable relationship to others—and especially to our weaker brethren—is one of love, and that means the will to hold fellowship with them. God himself did not despise humanity, but became man for men's sake.[5]

To a nephew who had joined the army in October 1942, he wrote:

> You know . . . the great blessings of a good family life, good parents, and also of justice and truth, humanity and culture, tradition. . . . But it is evident, and you know this yourself, that you will be brought face to face with conflicts—not merely with what is vulgar in itself, whose power you will be horrified to estimate in the coming weeks—but with the simple fact that, in coming from such a family, you are different from most other people, even in minor and superficial details. What matters is that your superiority . . . should be seen not as some merit of your own, but as a free gift, and that you should place yourself and everything you have at the service of others; that you should genuinely love them despite all the differences.[6]

In prison he was horrified by the trouble some of the gaolers took to give him special treatment as soon as they discovered what kind of family he came from.[7]

What Bonhoeffer was attached to was not any superiority of class. The nobility he stood for was a quality of mind rather than of name or race. In the manuscript I have just quoted he sees this new nobility showing itself, quite independent of national or class barriers, among the very people whom the national socialist régime had set out to dehumanize.

> We are witnessing the levelling down of all ranks of society, and at the same time the birth of a new sense of nobility, which is binding together a circle of men from all former social classes. Nobility arises from and exists by sacrifice, courage, and a clear sense of duty to oneself and society, by expecting due regard for

[5] *Ibid.*, 32.

[6] *Gesammelte Schriften* (4 vols, Munich, 1958-61), II, 424 (hereafter referred to as *G.S.*).

[7] *Letters and Papers from Prison*, 82.

itself as a matter of course; and it shows an equally natural regard for others, whether they are of higher or lower degree. . . . Quality is the greatest enemy of any kind of mass-levelling. Socially it means the renunciation of all place-hunting, a break with the cult of the 'star', an open eye both upwards and downwards, especially in the choice of one's more intimate friends, and pleasure in private life as well as courage to enter public life. Culturally it means a return from the newspaper and the radio to the book, from the feverish activity to unhurried leisure, from dispersion to concentration, from sensationalism to reflection, from virtuosity to art, from snobbery to modesty, from extravagance to moderation.[8]

One of the things Bonhoeffer most hated was folly. He dedicates a whole section of this same manuscript to it, and in a sense it is a summary of the principles of humanism upon which his own life was, of set choice, based. To him stupidity was not simply a failure of the mind. It was primarily a 'moral defect'.

There are people who are mentally agile but foolish, and people who are mentally slow but very far from foolish.[9]

Yet folly is generally not so much an inborn defect as the product of a given social order. It is perhaps 'a sociological rather than a psychological problem'. More precisely, 'it seems that any violent display of power, whether political or religious, produces an outburst of folly in a large part of mankind'. Apparently 'the power of some needs the folly of the others'. Folly, in other words, is a product of alienation. 'Folly can be overcome, not by instruction, but only by an act of liberation.'[10] Bonhoeffer's fight for a new nobility is really a fight for freedom. The only aristocracy he recognizes is that which is built upon the most basic human values.

A normal and richly human being

Just as his sense of human quality never led him to feel contempt for those less gifted than himself, so his taste and his

[8] ***Ibid.***, 35-6. [9] *Ibid.*, 31.
[10] ***Ibid.***

exceptional gifts for the intellectual life never made him insensitive or indifferent to the beauties and excellences of nature. His friend Eberhard Bethge says of him :

> He knew that a man could enjoy the beauty of this world while being ready to sacrifice it : [whether] the fruits of the earth, the warmth of the sun, friendships, fun, or wit. He was greatly drawn to people who could turn a meal into something special. He taught others how to celebrate a festivity. He could sacrifice all these things, yet even when sacrificing them, he loved to show others how to make the most of the beauties of the world.[11]

For instance, in a letter written in June 1944, he sings the praises of the wonderful power of the sun. In his prison cell he could picture the sufferings which his correspondent was suffering from the sun in Italy where he was fighting :

> And yet, you know, I should like to feel the full force of it (that sun) again, making the skin hot and the whole body aglow, and reminding me that I am a corporeal being. I should like to be tired by the sun, instead of by books and thoughts. I should like to have it awaken my animal existence—not the kind that degrades a man, but the kind that delivers him from the stuffiness and artificiality of a purely intellectual existence and makes him purer and happier. . . . Romantic sun-worshipping that just gets intoxicated over sunrise and sunset, while it knows something of the power of the sun, does not know it as a reality, but only as a symbol. It can never understand why people worshipped the sun as a god; to do so one needs experience, not only of light and colours, but also of heat.[12]

In other letters during the same period, he dwells on exciting memories of youth in the Harz mountains, the forests of Thuringia, the hills of the Weser.

Yet nothing could be more mistaken than to take this love of nature for any kind of naturalism. The passage I have just quoted on the enormous power of the sun reveals rather a man with a great sense of 'things', a man rooted in the physical reality of life. Bonhoeffer always felt a great distrust of idealist illusions, of any over-pure, disembodied intellectualism. He felt no more

[11] *Die mündige Welt*, I, 7.
[12] *Letters and Papers from Prison*, 187.

contempt for life and the world than he felt for men. The keen sense we find in him of God's transcendence and the agonizing demands of the gospel seems to have been authentic only in so far as it was related to a positive affirmation of the value of created being, and an active involvement in the history of the world. His Christian belief was never an other-worldly evangelism, nor did he ever envisage the glory of God as depending for its recognition upon the destruction of the creation. He loved the passionate love of the Song of Songs: 'It is a good thing that that book is in the Bible in face of all those who believe that the restraint of passion is Christian', he wrote.[13] It was certainly no fear of or contempt for the world that led him to decide, at sixteen, to become a pastor.

Before following him along this path, which will lead us to discover other traits of his character, it is relevant to note an impression emphasized by several of those who knew him well: the strange contrasts in his temperament and attitudes. These may certainly be seen as yet another aspect of his rich personality. But those impressions also point the way to something which I myself came to feel more keenly as my knowledge of Bonhoeffer and his work deepened: the impossibility of reducing the truth to which he bore witness, and to which he introduces us, to simply a few abstract principles or formulæ—which could in fact only travesty that truth.

One of his students writes:

> In all the notes I have made about him I find such phrases as: at once near and far, superiorly distant while at the same time open and available. A firm foundation linked with a controlled vitality. He was able to see beyond and transform such conflicts in an almost 'sacred' way.[14]

And Eberhard Bethge sums up his experience thus:

> An encounter with Bonhoeffer gave one the impression of a man who, in the liberty of faith, displayed the whole fullness of the *vita christiana*. In the course of a short life he had the gift of be-

[13] *Ibid.*, 162. [14] *Begegnung mit Bonhoeffer*, 51.

ing a man, a full man whose lord was Christ. One noted how opposites were harmonized in him. The intellectual was pious, and the pious man used his intellect. The scripture scholar was a boldly active man, and the active man remained a great scripture scholar. The pacifist became a conspirator, and the conspirator a pacifist. The German became a man beyond national loyalties, and the supranational man remained very German. The man of energy was shy and sensitive, and the shy man transformed those around him. Teaching, preaching and service of one's neighbours were inextricably linked together in his person.[15]

We shall now try to look at him in all these different areas.

A scholar and churchman

At sixteen, as I have said, Bonhoeffer decided to become a pastor. In 1923 he began his theological studies at Tübingen University, where he followed, among others, courses by the exegetes A. Schlatter and W. Heitmüller, and the dogmatist K. Hein. In addition to theology, he was initiated into modern philosophy.

The following year he enrolled at the university of Berlin, where he studied under Harnack, Deissmann and H. Lietzmann. Harnack was quick to recognize him as a promising theologian, and tried to persuade him to specialize in Church history. Though he did not follow his advice, Bonhoeffer always felt the deepest admiration for Harnack, who was 'a theologian and wanted to be a theologian', in other words, was wholly dedicated to the discipline whose purpose is to 'speak of God' (a theme he was to develop at a function in honour of the great scholar on 15 June, 1930).

Interested as he was in Church history, towards which Harnack wanted to lead him, Bonhoeffer was more interested still in systematic theology, as taught at that time in Berlin by two of those responsible for the renewal of Lutheran studies, K. Holl and R. Seeberg.

Like most theology students of the period, Bonhoeffer also

[15] *Die mündige Welt*, II, 103.

studied the early writings of Karl Barth; only later did he actually get to know him personally. But when he was able to be with him for a few weeks in Bonn in 1931, he wrote to his friend E. Sutz that he had 'rarely regretted any chance missed in his theological past as much as that of coming here sooner'.

> 'There is something here to see and to hear!' he declared enthusiastically. 'It is important, and surprising in the best way to see how Barth stands over and beyond his books . . . I have never seen anything like it before and wouldn't have believed it possible.'[16]

Meanwhile, however, in 1927, he had defended his doctoral thesis, under R. Seeberg, entitled *Sanctorum Communio.* I shall be discussing this work in the next chapter; for the moment we may at least indicate the interest Bonhoeffer showed in ecclesiological questions even at this early stage.

Nor was this interest then, or ever, exclusively a speculative one for him. We shall see, when we look at this first work, how his attention remained fixed upon the Church as it actually was, analysing both its human conditioning and its dimension of mystery. He did not rest content with simply studying the Church. Having finished his first stage at the university, he undertook a pastoral ministry. He was first of all a curate in the German parish in Barcelona. Returning to Berlin the following year (1929), he spent a large part of his time giving religious instruction and training to a group of adolescents in the working-class area of Wedding. He was also deeply concerned at the inhuman living conditions of his pupils' families and received his first initiation into social problems and practical economics. At first he ran into serious difficulties with these young people who 'at the beginning . . . behaved like mad things'. They had 'literally worried to death' all his predecessors. Yet it did not take him long to win them over, or in fact to be himself won over by them. His door was ever open, and all day long he would be visited by one group after another. They had recreation and meals together, and planned excursions. In the evening, they read and discussed the

[16] *G.S.*, I, 19-20 (*No Rusty Swords*, 121).

Bible, and he began to work out a new catechism based on 'the idea of community'.[17]

Nonetheless, Bonhoeffer managed to continue his own work as well. In 1930 he was ready to defend his thesis qualifying him for an academic career. The title of this in itself indicates how profoundly speculative it was, but also how essential was the standpoint from which he carried out his reflections: *Act and Being. Transcendental philosophy and ontology in systematic theology (Akt und Sein. Tranzendentalphilosophie und Ontologie in der systematischen Theologie)*. We shall see how this work complements the ecclesiological study in *Sanctorum Communio* and sets out to answer the vital questions of the time—some of which remain important in our own day.

But before taking on a university teaching job, Bonhoeffer decided to spend a further year studying at the Union Theological Seminary in New York. America did not simply bring him into contact with a whole new social, political and cultural world. He studied its problems, especially the negro problem, spending a lot of time in Harlem. But he also found there a Christian culture totally different from the one in which he had been brought up, a 'Protestantism without a Reformation', as he put it. He made some firm friendships there and developed a far more ecumenical outlook, having glimpsed the mammoth dimensions of the work to be done. In an account he wrote shortly afterwards (1932), he declared:

> The dogmatic differences between different Protestant Churches engaging in ecumenical work were more considerable than those between original Protestantism and Catholicism.[18]

He was from then on to play a major part in the various international organizations of the ecumenical movement. The many acquaintances he made in the course of this work, as also during his first American visit, were to enable him to become an effective force in helping the 'Confessing Church' in Germany avoid

[17] *G.S.*, I, 24-8 (*ibid.*, 139-41, 149-52).
[18] *G.S.*, I, 126 (*ibid.*, 178).

total isolation once the national socialist régime started to turn the country more and more in upon itself.

For his great openness to ecumenical and international affairs never prevented Bonhoeffer from remaining deeply preoccupied with the fate of his own country which, as he saw more clearly than anyone, was entering upon a path of total disaster. He was in Berlin again at the time of Hitler's rise to power. He had returned there in 1931 and begun teaching at the university. Through his sermons and personal contacts his influence on the students extended far beyond the strictly intellectual sphere.

Furthermore, his influence soon spread well beyond the limits of the university, and this exposed him to the danger that was seriously threatening the whole German Church. The national socialist régime provoked the disapproval of his Christian conscience from the start. As early as February 1933, he gave a radio lecture in which he criticized the people's longing to find a *Führer*, on the grounds that he was all too likely to become a *Verführer*, in other words a seducer, an idol. The broadcast was stopped half way.

As with so many others, it was the famous 'Arian paragraph' which really convinced him of the basic evil of the régime's programme and the need to oppose it firmly. After that there remained no ambiguity to justify hesitation. The famous 'paragraph' in fact was not only an attack upon everyone of Jewish race, but was to bring its injustice right into the Christian Church too, by destroying the brotherhood that was part of its essence. By excluding Christians of Jewish origin from the community, by forbidding Jews to be ordained pastors, the decree was in flat opposition to the clear teaching of the New Testament. Bonhoeffer realized that resistance would call for heavy sacrifices and indeed for heroism, and that there would be those for whom the struggle was too great. Obviously one must consider those of little faith, yet one cannot make 'the law of the weak the law of the Church'. For what was at issue here was something involving the very 'substance' of that Church. Without hesitation, therefore, he proposed an 'evangelical council' to 'decide between unity and schism for the Church'.[19] Though the actual term 'council' was not used again, the synods of Barmen and Dahlem (in 1934) were precisely that, setting out the doctrinal basis for what was to be called the 'Confessing Church' as opposed to the official Church of 'German Christians', which was totally enslaved to the ideology and underhand dealings of national socialism.

Henceforth Bonhoeffer's thoughts and actions alike were increasingly centred upon the life, needs and problems of this Confessing Church. It filled his teaching and his sermons, but it also entered into the work he still did abroad, and the part he played within the international institutions of the ecumenical movement.

In the autumn of 1933, in fact, he went to London, where he was offered the responsibility for two German parishes. Faced with a very complex situation, and caught in a rush of events, he felt the need to withdraw somewhat in order to prepare himself for a more self-assured, and hence more effective, form of action. It was a decision he made not without some hesitation. He realized that his choice was open to question, and only resolved to inform Karl Barth of it after he had made it. Nor indeed did Barth ever see the value of a step which looked to him simply like jumping off a moving train. Surrounded, however, by colleagues who, while just as anxious not to betray their trust, were often none too clear in their own minds, Bonhoeffer felt 'interiorly insecure' and rather isolated. He tried with some difficulty to write what he felt to Barth from England:

> I thought that it was probably time to go into the wilderness for a while and simply do pastoral work, with as little demand as possible. The danger of making a gesture at the present moment seemed to me greater than that of going off for some quietness . . . I am infinitely glad to be among a congregation, even so completely out of things.

And, he says: 'I have always very much wanted to become a pastor.'[20]

Finally, he thought that during this stay in England, 'the ques-

[19] *G.S.*, II, 55. [20] *G.S.*, II, 126-34 (*ibid.*, 230-40).

tions about the ecumenical movement will really clear themselves up for me'. He could see that the terrible problems the Evangelical Church in Germany was having to face must necessarily have repercussions on the whole ecumenical movement. He intended, he says, to 'carry on here the work' of building up the Confessing Church on an ecumenical scale. And in fact, 'perhaps in this way one can really support the German Church once again in something.'[21] In any case, he made a great many contacts, and in particular, he shared in several of the Anglican experiments in community life.

But Barth continued to see things differently. And when Bonhoeffer went on to ask his opinion, he said frankly:

> As you are mentioning the matter to me *post eventum,* I can honestly not tell you anything but 'Hurry back to your post in Berlin!' What is all this about 'going away', 'the quietness of pastoral work', etc., at a moment when you are just wanted in Germany? . . . Don't you see yet that an age of completely undialectical theology has dawned in which it just won't do to keep oneself in reserve with a 'Perhaps—but again, perhaps not'? Don't you see that any biblical saying you like formally cries out to us that we, lost and damned sinners, should now simply believe, believe, believe?! . . . You must now leave go of all these intellectual flourishes and special considerations, however interesting they may be, and think of only one thing, that you are a German, that the house of your church is on fire, that you know enough and can say what you know well enough to be able to help and that you must return to your post by the next ship. As things are, shall we say the ship after next?[22]

Bonhoeffer did not act quite so quickly. Barth's letter was dated 20 November 1933. He stayed in London until the spring of 1935. He did, however, go back to Germany several times during that period, to take part in conferences and study groups of various organizations within the Confessing Church. He also took part in Paris in a session of the 'ecumenical commission for youth', went to the international conference of youth at Fanö, and spent a few days at Bruay-en-Artois with his friend Jean Lasserre

[21] *G.S.*, II, 133 (*ibid.*, 236). [22] *G.S.*, II, 134-7 (*ibid.*, 237-9).

(whom he had got to know in New York). On the other hand, he had to give up a journey to India and a longed-for meeting with Gandhi which an English friend had arranged for him.

An educator and pastor

Indeed, it was while preparing for that journey that he was called by the authorities of the Confessing Church to take in hand the establishment and direction of a pastoral seminary to be established at Zingst, on the Baltic. From Zingst, where the material conditions of life were far too uncertain, the seminary soon moved to Finkenwalde, near Stettin, and there it remained until its dissolution by Himmler in October 1937.

In the 'community of brethren' at Finkenwalde, Bonhoeffer established with his students what really amounted to a conventual life—a point soon noticed by critics against whom he had to defend it. There was prayer in common, study, fraternal correction and finally confession, the celebration of the Lord's supper, and periods of delightful relaxation in the neighbouring hills: all this went to make up the 'common life' at Finkenwalde.[23] Another element was the experience of evangelical poverty. It was a time of exceptional fervour, stimulated by the realization of the hardships these future ministers of the gospel would be called upon to face. We find echoes of the meditations and discussions of this time in the two books *The Cost of Discipleship*, and *Life Together*, published respectively in 1937 and 1938, to which I shall be returning in detail in a later chapter. His short introduction to meditation on the psalms, *Das Gebetbuch der Bibel*, and the little book *Versuchung* (Temptation) also give us an idea of the kind of biblical study he was so fond of.

This latter work contains the conferences from a day of recollection. For, while animating the life of the seminary at all levels, Bonhoeffer also very often welcomed neighbouring pastors to his house, as well as former students now doing parish work or in the

[23] Cf *G.S.*, II, 454 (*The Way to Freedom*, 36). See also *Life Together* which examines this experience at depth.

army. During the war he kept up with those on active service—and eventually with their families—a copious correspondence, some individually, some collectively. A certain number of these letters and circulars have been preserved. When he first began his ministry in Berlin, Bonhoeffer had noted that to be able to carry out the pastoral ministry it was not enough just to have learnt to preach; what was involved was more precisely what the Germans call *Seelsorge*, or in our old-fashioned term, the 'care of souls'.[24] His letters from Finkenwalde reveals a *Seelsorger*, a 'spiritual Father', of unusual authority, profundity and sensitivity.

In a letter to Karl Barth, on 19 September 1936, he expresses his conviction of the prime importance of the spiritual training of future ministers.

> On an opening evening . . . you once said very seriously to the students that you sometimes felt as though you would rather give up all lectures and instead pay a surprise visit on someone and ask him, like old Tholuck, 'How goes it with your soul?' . . . But there are very few who recognize this sort of work for young theologians as a task of the church and do something about it. . . . Unfortunately I am not up to it, but I remind the brothers of each other, and that seems to me to be the most important thing. It is, though, certain that both theological work and real pastoral fellowship can only grow in a life which is governed by gathering round the Word morning and evening and by fixed times of prayer. . . . A leading man in the Confessing Church recently said to me: 'We have no time for meditation now, the ordinands should learn how to preach and catechise.' That seems to me either a complete misunderstanding of what young theologians are like to day, or a culpable ignorance of how preaching and catechism come to life.[25]

He works out this theme of the prime importance of daily meditation in a circular letter to the 'brothers', dated 1 March 1942:

> The daily, silent meditation upon the Word of God with which I am concerned—even if it is only for a few minutes—must be for me the crystallization of everything that brings order into my life,

[24] *G.S.*, I, 29 (*No Rusty Swords*, 151).
[25] *G.S.*, II 285-6 (*The Way to Freedom*, 117-18).

both inwardly and outwardly. In these days when our old rules of life have had to be discarded, and there is great danger of finding our inner order endangered by the rush of events, and by the all-absorbing demands of work and service, meditation gives our life a kind of stability, maintaining a link with our earlier life, from baptism to confirmation and ordination, preserving us in the saving way of communion and community, with our brothers, with our spiritual home; it is a spark of that fire which the communities want to keep alive here for you, a source of peace, patience and joy, a magnet drawing all the resources of order at our disposal, a pure and deep-welling water in which heaven, with its clouds and its sunshine, is clearly reflected.[26]

Yet he was aware that life at the front could not be the same as life at Finkenwalde, and spoke as forcefully of inward freedom as of fidelity. Thus, in a personal letter in May 1940, he explains that, while one must always remain aware of one's responsibility as a Christian and never betray one's ministry, it is neither necessary nor even, in many cases, desirable to think of oneself as always 'on duty':

I think the time has come again to say something about freedom in our Christian life and about God's grace. . . . I do not know whether it is right to keep repeating to you that you are and must be, even when you are so far away, 'on duty'. Obviously, none of us is ever quit of the responsibility that goes with being a Christian, nor must we ever renounce our quality as ministers. But it is surely something rather different to assume that one must be, even there, 'on duty'. It seems to me that you are not, nor could you be. . . . In this matter we must guard carefully against high and mighty ideas which may perhaps be all very fine for a time, but can one day become highly dangerous and destroy everything we believe. . . . As a soldier one cannot simply carry on as a pastor, and one should not be inwardly tormented by the fact.[27]

Bonhoeffer goes on to formulate a few ideas which are an earlier adumbration of the famous reflections we find in the letters from prison. Of those who are tormented by their inability to do anything that seems like a ministry or even to have any influence on conversations that are anything but spiritual, he writes:

[26] *G.S.*, II, 584-5. [27] *G.S.*, I, 566.

Of course it would be marvellous to be able to have some effect on what those around us say, on what they talk about. But once again, I do not believe that it is good or desirable to cultivate too great a sensitivity in oneself, for it may only make us more helpless and even less able to give assistance of a more definite kind. If you have learnt to know in the cross of Christ the power and the ways of the world, with all the evil that goes with them, and if at the same time you truly believe in God's love for that world, then you should not after all be too surprised or overwhelmed by the ways in which the reality of that world is expressed.[28]

Those exposed to the dangers of active service and experiencing all the human sufferings to be found there were not the only people who needed advice and encouragement. There were some who suffered from the opposite sense of being spared those things, and being condemned to a life of emptiness. What matters, Bonhoeffer explains, is to be conformed to the will of God, and ready to fulfil whatever mission is required of one.

At every moment, wherever he may be, there are plenty of dangers, experiences, and trials for any Christian who really knows what his faith means. If God, in his graciousness, allows our fighting, wounded and dying brothers in the front line to witness those extraordinary and fearful experiences being transformed into blessings, we should be failing in respect for that miracle if we were to want such experiences for ourselves without their being required of us. Who knows how he would behave under them? Who wants to tempt God? God knows what he can ask of us, and he will quite certainly ask it, in his own good time. We must simply be ready for that time, while trying daily to measure up humbly and faithfully to the dangers and trials that fall to our own lot.[29]

Yet death kept striking his 'brothers' as more and more of them became involved in the war. It provided the constant theme for Bonhoeffer's letters to those in grief. A young pastor died during the Polish campaign in September 1939. Bonhoeffer wrote of him in a general letter to his former comrades. He added:

Where God tears great gaps we should not try to fill them with human words. Our only comfort is the God of the resurrection,

[28] *G.S.*, II, 567. [29] *G.S.*, II, 581.

the Father of our Lord Jesus Christ who also was and is his God. In him we know our brothers and in him is the abiding fellowship of those who have overcome and those who still await their hour. God be praised for our dead brother and be merciful to us all at the end.[30]

He writes of another young pastor who died on the Russian front in 1942:

With his death, something of the light of Christ has gone out, that light we are occasionally allowed to glimpse through a human being; but it is only in order that that light may shine more brightly than ever in the eternal sun of Jesus Christ.[31]

And Bonhoeffer progressively leads his correspondents deeper into the mystery of death which is something we find especially disconcerting when it strikes those who are young and full of promise, and of whom we tend to think that God is wrong to deprive himself. Our first duty is to silence the claims of our rational understanding.

We must rein in our human ideas when they want to know more than they can take in, and must cling only to what we know for sure. The man God calls to himself is the man he has loved. 'His soul was pleasing to the Lord, therefore he took him quickly from the midst of wickedness' (Wisd 4:14).[32]

This was no mere fatalism, still less any love of death for its own sake, for death is God's enemy too. Rather, we must recognize in it a tragic ambiguity, explainable only by faith in the dead and risen Christ.

We know very well that God and the devil are in conflict in the world, and that the devil's world is also being heard in death. When we see death, we cannot adopt the stance of fatalism, declaring: 'God wills it', unless we add in the same breath: 'God does not will it'. Death shows that the world is not as it should be, that it needs redemption. Christ is the only victory over death. In him the two statements—'God wills it' and 'God does not will it'—are wholly true. . . . Only in the cross and resurrection of Jesus Christ

[30] *G.S.*, II, 553 (*The Way to Freedom*, 251). [31] *G.S.*, II, 574-5.
[32] *G.S.*, II, 576.

> does death fall under the power of God and serve his ends. It is no fatalist resignation, but faith in Christ dead and risen for us, that enables us truly to overcome the mystery of death.[33]

While recalling these important truths, Bonhoeffer never forgot how inadequate human words are to cope with a reality which, in the circumstances of those extraordinary years, was more resistant than ever to every assault of the mind and all too likely to baffle all faith. His sense of unworthiness became more and more profound. We shall find it developed still further in the letters from prison. His life and everything he said became ever more concentrated upon one name only, the name of Christ Jesus.

> Dear brothers, it may be that you now have little time or freedom to consider such ideas. There are moments when all of reality becomes so enigmatic and so oppressive that any direct word seems to destroy the mystery, and we want only to speak—and hear—of the last things by illusion. Anything we are able to say about our faith then seems so dreary and meaningless in comparison with the reality we are experiencing, a reality behind which we believe an inexpressable mystery to be present. In this we at home feel almost the same as you out there; all we can say is no more than the brief winking of an eye; what we can put into words no longer coincides with reality. This can be an extremely authentic recognition, as long as there is one word which we always hang on to—the name of Jesus Christ. That name remains a word, the Word around which all our words revolve. In that word alone we find illumination and strength. 'In the depths of my heart there shines only thy Name and thy Cross, at all seasons, at all moments. On that my joy can be fed.'[34]

Inflexible in resistance

In October 1937, the pastoral seminary at Finkenwalde was closed by order of the Gestapo. The following month, twenty-seven of its former students were in prison. The work went on for some time in concealment, but the régime gradually became harsher, and Bonhoeffer was soon forbidden not merely to teach,

[33] *Ibid.*

[34] *G.S.*, II, 577. The reference is to a hymn.

but to publish as well. Freedom in Germany became more and more hampered, and this fact certainly contributed to making him accept the invitation of his friends in America to undertake a lecture tour there beginning in June 1939. It provided the further advantage of enabling him to avoid enlistment.

However he began almost at once to feel uneasy at being so far away from his brothers in Germany who remained in suffering and danger. He could not resign himself to being cut off from them and in safety if war, which now seemed inevitable, meant the closing of all frontiers. He began to feel the situation unbearable. His shipboard journal and a few letters show us what agonies of conscience he was undergoing. He wrote to Reinhold Niebuhr:

> Sitting here in Dr Coffin's garden, I have had the time to think and pray about my situation and that of my nation and to have God's will for me clarified. I have come to the conclusion that I have made a mistake in coming to America. I must live through this difficult period of our national history with the Christian people of Germany. I will have no right to participate in the reconstruction of Christian life in Germany after the war if I do not share the trials of this time with my people.

He goes on to speak of the terrible dilemma in which some of his compatriots are finding themselves:

> Christians in Germany will face the terrible alternative of either willing the defeat of their nation in order that Christian civilization may survive or willing the victory of their nation and thereby destroying our civilization.[35]

Despite pressure from his friends, he was on his way back to Berlin on 27 July, six weeks after having left it. From prison, some years later, he was to say several times that he had never regretted the decision.

> Now I want to assure you that I have not for a moment regretted coming back in 1939. . . . I knew quite well what I was doing, and I acted with a clear conscience. I have no wish to cross out of my life anything that has happened since. . . . And I? my being kept

[35] *G.S.*, I, 320 (*The Way to Freedom*, 246).

here . . . as being involved in the part that I had resolved to play in Germany's fate. It is with no reproach that I look back on the past and accept the present.[36]

During the three and a half years in which he still had relative freedom of action, Bonhoeffer did a considerable amount. He was still able to give some time to the 'brotherly counselling' of the Confessing Church, and provide some help to pastors in Pomerania. Though he had no immediate hope of publishing it, he worked steadily on compiling his *Ethics*, a book very dear to his heart; it was eventually published, posthumously and unfinished, after the war by Bethge. He became more and more involved in the movement of active resistance to Hitler. And—astonishing for a man so suspect in the eyes of the régime—he managed to get official permits (no doubt with a certain amount of 'unofficial help) to leave wartime Germany several times, and thus maintain very important links with foreign representatives of the ecumenical movement.

From 17 November 1940 until 23 February 1941, he retreated to the Benedictine abbey of Ettal in the Bavarian mountains. He stayed in the guest-house, but ate in the monks' refectory and had a set of keys to the cloister and library. He took advantage of these splendid conditions for working, and made great advances with his *Ethics*. In various letters to family and friends, he described his impressions of the monastic life. It was not, he said a way of life 'foreign' to him, and he found it favourable to peace and hard work.

It would certainly be a loss (and indeed it was a loss at the Reformation!) if community life, which has proved its worth over the past fifteen hundred years, were to be destroyed; they fear here that this is possible.[37]

The *recto tono* reading in the refectory struck him as curious, but he thought the principle of reading in so large a community was 'not such a bad thing'. He even enjoyed assisting at the conventual Mass.

[36] *Letters and Papers from Prison*, 115; cf. 149. [37] *G.S.*, II, 382.

I have just come from a wonderful Mass. With missal in hand, one can very largely join in the prayer, and that with no reservations. It is certainly not idolatory. However, this road from our sacrifice offered to God and God's sacrifice for us I do not like much, and it seems to me a false one. But I must get to understand it better. I am still a guest here. Living according to a rule again is doing me great good, and I find it astonishing how naturally we ourselves did something so very similar. Also the Father Abbot and several of the other fathers here have read 'Of community life', and we are to discuss it together soon. The absolutely spontaneous hospitality which is clearly something specifically Benedictine, and the deeply Christian respect shown to outsiders, all this is almost overwhelming.[38]

During the early years of the Nazi dictatorship, Bonhoeffer took part chiefly in the spiritual resistance of the Confessing Church. There he was always among the most intransigent. '*Extra ecclesiam nulla salus* . . . to cut oneself off knowingly from the Confessing Church is to cut oneself off from salvation', he said bluntly in 1936.[39] And he intended equally definitely to make the ecumenical council face up to its responsibilities, by forcing it to choose between the Confessing Church and the official Church of German Christians.

However, such spiritual resistance did not in the end seem to him enough. He appears, from 1938 onwards, to have been in touch with those who were working for the overthrow of the régime by force. He was chiefly initiated into their plans by his brother-in-law, Hans von Dohnanyi, a close colleague of General Beck, head of the *Abwehr* and mainspring of the military resistance. When one of his fellow-prisoners, an Italian, asked him during the short exercise the prisoners took in the prison-yard how he, as a Christian and a minister, could have taken part in a conspiracy, Bonhoeffer, who could hardly under the circumstances launch into any long explanations, simply replied :

If a lunatic drove his car on to the pavement in the Kurfürstendam, I could not, as a minister, rest content with burying the dead

[38] *G.S.*, II, 383-4. [39] *G.S.*, II, 238. Cf. *infra*, p. 57.

and consoling their relations. I should have, if I were present, to rush forward and prevent the driver from getting away.[40]

In the same way, he declared once: 'Only a man who will speak out in favour of the Jews has any right to sing Gregorian chant.'[41]

In September 1941, he went to Geneva to meet Pastor Visser 't Hooft, then Secretary General of the World Council of Churches. His purpose was in the first place to get into touch with the Englishmen in the group, to let them know the movements planned by the German resistance after the fall of Hitler. It was in every way a dangerous undertaking. It was not easy to get past the Basle frontiers, since the Swiss police were anxious to make sure that they were not letting a Hitler agent through into their territory. To reassure them, Bonhoeffer telephoned Karl Barth, asking him to guarantee him. But Barth had heard nothing of Bonhoeffer for some time, and was somewhat doubtful, so that it was only with difficulty that he acceded to his old friend's request. This was typical of the impossible situation in which those Germans who wanted to dissociate themselves from their country's criminal behaviour were placed.

Bonhoeffer was to have a second, even more agonizing, experience of this when he left, a second time, to go to Sweden in May 1942. It was Bishop Bell of Chichester, President of the World Council of Churches, whom he was to meet there. They had been close friends since his stay in London in 1933, and the Bishop felt no reservations about Bonhoeffer's intentions. The disappointment came later. Bishop Bell's major task was to act as intermediary with the English government; in the end he handed two detailed memoranda to Anthony Eden, the foreign secretary, one which he had himself compiled, the other compiled by H. Schönefeld, who had gone with Bonhoeffer to Stockholm and was informing the English government about the activity, the plans, and the names of the leaders of the chief resistance movements inside the Reich. In addition, there was the question of what support the Allies might decide to give the activities being

[40] *Die mündige Welt*, I, 14. [41] *Ibid.*, 23.

undertaken inside Germany: might they at least hope to find those of the German people who were fighting as best they could, in very difficult circumstances, dissociated from that Nazi Germany which the Allies were determined to obliterate? Bishop Bell did not manage to meet Eden in person, but put the matter to him fervently by letter; his plea however met with rejection. Eden was quite ready to believe in the good faith of the two pastors Bell spoke of, but went on to declare his conviction that 'it would not be in the national interest to send them any reply'.[42] To the urgings of Bell, he explained in a further letter, that he knew 'the dangers and difficulties threatening the opposition in Germany', but that those in opposition had not, in his view, given sufficient evidence of the effectiveness of their plans. In other words, the resistants must accept the fact that they would receive no promises, no real encouragement, until they had actually overthrown Hitler. Meanwhile they could only work in the dark.

That darkness was to take a more positive form for Bonhoeffer on 5 April 1943, when he was arrested by the Gestapo at his parents' house in Berlin, a few hours after his brother-in-law Hans von Dohnanyi.

'A witness to Jesus Christ among his brothers'

This inscription, engraved on the memorial tablet in the church at Flossenbürg, where he was executed, expresses what Bonhoeffer always was. But in the final months of his life, which we need only mention briefly here, it became truer than ever before.

From the military section of the Tegel prison in Berlin, where he spent the first eight months of his captivity, Bonhoeffer wrote a number of letters, which were legally permitted and duly censored, to his parents. But in addition, with the complicity of some of the warders and prison-cleaners, he was able to keep up a clandestine correspondence as well—in particular with his fiancée Maria von Wedemeyer, and his friend Eberhard Bethge. The letters to his fiancée have not been made public, but those to

[42] *G.S.*, I, 384.

Bethge, several of those to his parents, and various other documents have been put together into a book which has drawn the whole world's attention to the name of Bonhoeffer; it is edited by Bethge, and was published under the title *Widerstand und Ergebung* (the English version being called simply *Letters and Papers from Prison*).[43] I shall come to consider this important book further in the next chapter, especially in regard to the ideas, later to have such a tremendous impact, about the 'non-religious interpretation' of the Christian faith as we are called to live it today in a 'world come of age'. Here, I shall simply note a few points which help to round off our knowledge of the man during this last part of his life, and to suggest how important is the witness he has left us.

At Tegel, Bonhoeffer shared the same living conditions as so many prisoners, of which we have already had many other accounts.[44] 'In more than one respect my time of imprisonment is being a very wholesome though drastic cure', he wrote on 29 November 1943.[45] He had bouts of depression, but was determined not to give way to them. He resolved to get up regularly at six, so as not to risk 'capitulating' even on so small a point.

> An outward and purely physical régime (exercises and a cold wash down in the morning) itself provides some support for one's inner discipline. . . . Another point : I don't think it is good to talk to strangers about our condition; that always stirs up one's troubles—although we ought to be ready, when the occasion arises, to listen to those of other people.[46]

He sought strength and peace not in any hardening of heart, but in the depths of a healthy realism, illumined by faith.

> Nothing can make up for the absence of someone whom we love, and it would be wrong to try to find a substitute; we must simply hold out and see it through. That sounds very hard at first, but at the same time it is a great consolation, for the gap as long as it

[43] The phrase, which means 'Resistance and Submission' comes from one of the letters.

[44] He himself wrote out a 'report' on the subject. Cf. *Letters and Papers from Prison*, 81-6.

[45] *Ibid.*, 102. [46] *Ibid.*, 110.

remains unfilled, preserves the bonds between us. It is nonsense to say that God fills the gap; he does not fill it, but on the contrary, he keeps it empty and so helps us to keep alive our former communion with each other, even at the cost of pain.[47]

As for our memories, which, delightful though they are, increase our sufferings, we must not let ourselves be tormented by them, but rather value them as a precious gift. And 'gratitude changes the pangs of memory into a tranquil joy'. Finally, notes Bonhoeffer, 'I have learnt here especially that the *facts* can always be mastered, and that difficulties are magnified out of all proportion simply by fear and anxiety.'[48]

For the rest, despite the material hardships, he continued to maintain an intense intellectual life. The reader is amazed at the breadth of his culture. His customary richness of life was in no way hampered by a situation in which everything conspired to destroy it; on the contrary, this only served to show its tremendous strength. He himself described that strength in a letter of 25 May 1944, which sums up his spiritual experience, together with that 'reserve' I spoke of earlier.

I hope that, in spite of the alarms, you are enjoying to the full the peace and beauty of those warm, summer-like Whitsuntide days. One gradually learns to acquire an inner detachment from life's menaces—although 'acquire detachment' seems too negative, formal, artificial, and stoical; and it is perhaps more accurate to say that we assimilate these menaces into our life as a whole. I notice repeatedly here how few people there are who can harbour conflicting emotions at the same time. When bombers come, they are all fear; when there is something nice to eat, they are all greed; when they are disappointed, they are all despair; when they are successful, they can think of nothing else. They miss the fullness of life and the wholeness of an independent existence; everything objective and subjective is dissolved for them into fragments.

It is given to us by the Christian faith to have such fullness and unity of life:

By contrast, Christianity puts us into many different dimensions of life at the same time; we make room in ourselves, to some

[47] *Ibid.*, 116. [48] *Ibid.*, 116-17.

extent, for God and the whole world. We rejoice with those who rejoice, and weep with those who weep; we are anxious (I was again interrupted just then by the alarm, and am now sitting out of doors enjoying the sun) about our life, but at the same time we must think about things much more important to us than life itself. When the alarm goes, for instance: as soon as we turn our minds from worrying about our own safety to the task of helping other people to keep calm, the situation is completely changed; life is not pushed back into a single dimension, but is kept multi-dimensional and polyphonous. What a deliverance it is to be able to *think*, and thereby remain multi-dimensional. I have almost made it a rule here, simply to tell people who are trembling under an air raid that it would be much worse for a small town. We have to get people out of their one-track minds; that is a kind of 'preparation' for faith, or something that makes faith possible, although really it is only faith itself that can make possible a multi-dimensional life, and so enable us to keep this Whistuntide too, in spite of the alarms.[49]

The attempt to kill Hitler that failed on 20 July 1944, and the discovery in September of papers which implicated the resistance group Bonhoeffer belonged to, resulted in his being moved from Tegel on 8 October to the dreaded Gestapo prison in the Prinz-Albert-Strasse in Berlin. From thenceforth all contacts with the world outside ceased. For that period we only have the accounts of some of his fellow-prisoners, especially of the man in the next cell, Fabian von Schlabrendorff.

Bonhoeffer told me about his interrogations, how he was first tortured, and how the interrogations were the sheerest blackmail. Outwardly he showed no emotion. He was always good-tempered, and his pleasant manner to everyone never varied—so much so that, to my surprise, even his warders fell under his spell. In our conversations, it was always he who remained hopeful, whereas I was sometimes deeply discouraged. He never tired of saying that the battle is only lost when you admit defeat. Often and often he would slip into my hand a scrap of paper with a few words of comfort and faith from the Bible written on it. He was always equally optimistic about his own situation.[50]

[49] *Ibid.*, 173-4.
[50] Quoted by J. D. Godsey in *The Theology of Dietrich Bonhoeffer*, London, 1960.

One February day in 1945, he was taken away from Prinz-Albert-Strasse. His family heard no more news of him until after the armistice. We have, however some scraps of information about his last days from some of those who were with him but were not eventually executed.

He was taken first to Buchenwald, where he met 'special' prisoners from all over Europe, including the aviator Vassili Kokorin, Molotov's nephew, from whom he began to learn Russian, while teaching him something about Christianity. He also exercised his pastoral ministry for any one who wished it. An officer in the British Intelligence Service, Payne Best, wrote of his memories of the time:

> Bonhoeffer . . . was all humility and sweetness; he always seemed to me to diffuse an atmosphere of happiness, of joy, in every smallest event in life, and of deep gratitude for the mere fact that he was alive. . . . He was one of the few men that I have met to whom God was real and close.[51]

To this we may add the account of a Rabbi who did not know Bonhoeffer, but wrote to Bethge after the publication of the *Letters and Papers from Prison*, that Bonhoeffer had made him understand for the first time how one might be able to worship Jesus Christ.[52] We may keep these comments in mind as we try to interpret the message contained in that book.

On Easter Tuesday 1945, Bonhoeffer and some other 'special' prisoners were put into an army truck that was to take them to the extermination camp at Flossenbürg. Their destination was changed half way, however. The prisoners were unloaded on the Wednesday in the Bavarian village of Schönberg and locked in the school.

The following Sunday, Low Sunday, one of the prisoners asked Bonhoeffer to officiate at a morning service. At first he refused; most of those present were Catholics, and he felt that it would not be tactful. Nor did he want to embarrass young Kokorin. But

[51] This account is quoted by Eberhard Bethge in his Foreword to the *Letters and Papers from Prison*, p. 24.

[52] *Die mündige Welt*, I, 9.

Kokorin said he would like it, and the whole group agreed. Bonhoeffer therefore held a service of the Word: the texts from the Sunday's liturgy were read, there were prayers, and a sermon on the day's texts (Is 53:5 and 1 Pet 1:3). The families of some important resistance members, who were lodged in the next room, planned to get Bonhoeffer through to them secretly so as to hold another service there. But before they could begin to put their plan into effect, the door was pushed open and two men in civilian clothes called: 'Prisoner Bonhoeffer, get ready to come with us.' He gathered up his things, wrote his name and the name of the village on a piece of paper which he slipped into a copy of Plutarch that he had with him, and left it purposely behind on the table. One of the sons of Goerdeler, the leader of the political resistance, picked it up and gave it to his family after the war. Bonhoeffer finally asked Payne Best to remember him to the Bishop of Chichester, and on leaving the room, he said: 'This is the end. For me the beginning of life.' The next morning, 9 April, at the age of 39, he was hanged.

He had himself, shortly before, explained how such lives, though cut short prematurely, may fulfil their purpose:

> There are some fragments that are only worth throwing into the dustbin (even a decent 'hell' is too good for them), and others whose importance lasts for centuries, because their completion can only be a matter for God, and so they are fragments that must be fragments—I am thinking, e.g., of the *Art of Fugue*. If our life is but the remotest reflection of such a fragment, if we accumulate, at least for a short time, a wealth of themes and weld them into a harmony in which the great counterpoint is maintained from the start to finish, so that at last, when it breaks off abruptly, we can sing no more than the chorale, *Vor deinen Thron tret' ich allhier*, we will not bemoan the fragmentariness of our life, but rather rejoice in it.[53]

[53] *Letters and Papers from Prison*, 135.

II

A Theologian of the Church and of Christ

In Dietrich Bonhoeffer's theological thinking, prematurely cut short, the Church always held pride of place. He made it the subject of his first major systematic work, his doctoral thesis of 1927 : *Sanctorum Communio*. But it was also to provide a firmer basis for his fundamental intuitions that he wrote, in 1931, his 'qualifying' thesis for higher education : *Akt und Sein (Act and Being)*. In more limited studies, intended primarily to answer questions arising from the establishment of the Confessing Church, and also from his ecumenical work, he continued to enlarge upon various aspects of his ecclesiological teaching. And the thought of the Church, its situation and its mission in the world of the future, remained the dominant note of his meditations in prison. These last can be understood best against the background of his early studies and views, which are also well worth considering for their own sake, for in many ways they were prophetic at the time of writing and still preserve an amazing relevance in our own day.

The Church as a concrete reality

When Bonhoeffer defended his thesis in 1927, the renewal of ecclesiology which marks our time had barely begun, especially among Protestants. Even now, we are not yet fully aware of its importance. In the preface he wrote for the new edition of *Sanctorum Communio* in 1954, E. Wolf rightly pointed out that it represented 'among the relatively few recent monographs on ecclesiology, the most penetrating and perhaps most profound study of the problem of the constitutive structure of the Church'. Bonhoeffer, he goes on to explain, approaches what is undoubtedly the most essential question, that of knowing 'whether and how the empirical Church and the Church in its true nature can, from the logical, sociological and theological point of view be brought together in a single concept.'[1]

The sub-title he gave his book gives us a glimpse of the originality of what he was trying to do at that time: 'A dogmatic inquiry into the sociology of the Church.' The German word *Soziologie* is not, in fact, quite synonymous with our 'sociology', for the latter indicates a positive science with fairly clearly defined rules, the German word usually suggests something wider or more abstract, involving the whole theory of society and social phenomena. Thus Bonhoeffer could accurately describe the viewpoint of his study as 'dogmatic', though that dogmatic study made use of 'social philosophy and sociology'.[2]

In his introduction he recalls 'the social intention of all the basic Christian concepts. . . . "Person", "primal state", "sin" and "revelation" are fully understandable only in relation to sociality.' They are, in other words, so many 'social aspects of dogma', and Bonhoeffer was here attempting to throw light upon them, as Henri de Lubac was to do ten years later in *Catholicisme*.[3] Thus a whole section of the book is devoted to analyzing the chief concepts which can illuminate a 'sociology of the Church': 'the person', the 'I-Thou relationship', 'social community', 'objective spirit', and so on. These considerations, though reflective in nature, never led the author to forget that 'the reality of the Church is a reality of revelation.'[4] 'The Church', he declares, 'is founded in the revelation of God's heart.'[5] Bonhoeffer makes no attempt to arrive at dogma by deduction; he starts with the revealed and existing reality of the Church in his quest for its 'inner logic'.[6]

One theme that runs through the whole study is 'Christ existing

[1] Wolf's preface does not appear in the English edition (*S.C.*, 5).
[2] *Sanctorum Communio*, 13, 19.
[3] H. de Lubac, *Catholicisme, Les aspects sociaux du dogme*, Paris, 1938.
[4] *Sanctorum Communio*, 89.
[5] *Ibid.*, 87. [6] *Ibid.*, 97.

as the Church'.[7] Bonhoeffer did not mean to develop any kind of totalitarian conception of the Church as inspired by the romantic mystique of the *Jugendbewegung* (youth movement) still so popular in Germany at the time. He warns us against doing this:

> If we now ask at what point faith most purely 'experiences the Church', then the answer is that this certainly does not come about in the communities built upon a romantic feeling of solidarity between kindred spirits, but rather when there is nothing but the Church community linking the individuals concerned, where Jew and Greek, Pietist and Liberal come into conflict and nevertheless profess their faith in unity, nevertheless come together for Holy Communion and intercede for one another in prayer; it is precisely in the commonplace surroundings of every day that the Church is believed and experienced; it is not in moments of spiritual exaltation, but in the monotony and severity of daily life, and in the regular worship of God that we come to understand the Church's full significance. All else merely veils the true state of things. . . . Our age is not poor in experiences, but in faith. Only faith can create true experience of the Church, so we think it more important for our age to be led into belief in the Church of God, than to have experiences squeezed from it which as such are of no help at all, but which when there is faith in the *sanctorum communio*, are produced of their own accord.[8]

Just as the experience of the Church is a product of faith, so the 'personal unity' of the Church comes to it from its head, Jesus Christ.[9] But Christ must be studied in all the dimensions that faith reveals to us in him. He is the new Adam, and in him creation finds its purpose and fulfilment. Furthermore, the Church, brought together through and in him, can never be seen simply as a 'means' whose only significance and value exists in relation to an end outside itself. It also has its own inner goal *(Selbstzweck)*. 'It is the presence of Christ himself.' And that is why 'being in Christ', which is the definition of Christian life, is the same as 'being in the Church'.[10]

It is indeed, then, in the concrete and historical community of

[7] Cf. *ibid.*, 85, 100-2, 135-6, 139, 143, 145, 147, 149, 160, 180, 197, 203.
[8] *Ibid.*, 197-8. [9] *Ibid.*, 138.
[10] *Ibid.*, 135.

believers that union with Christ and with God takes place. Bonhoeffer does not hesitate to defend the sociological Church, the 'national Church', the *Volkskirche*, against those who want to replace it by a 'gathered Church' *(Freiwilligkeitskirche)*.[11] In this connection he condemned the resentment which it is all too easy for the faithful to feel towards their Church, and the 'dogmatic frivolousness' that so often precedes it. Obviously one cannot purely and simply identify 'the objective spirit of the collective person of the Church . . . with the Holy Spirit'. But that objective spirit, what we would call the *sensus fidelium*, the consciousness of the Christian people as such, is the 'object and means of operation of the Holy Spirit'.[12]

It is from this character and this role that the Church's authority flows, not simply in matters of doctrine, but also when it takes up an 'attitude to contemporary events and to the world at large'. It can require us to make a *sacrificium intellectus*, or even on occasion a *sacrificium conscientiae*, though its authority will always remain relative as compared with the absolute authority of the Word of God.[13]

The ecclesial teaching of *Sanctorum Communio* is thus very far from any return to the conception or the ideal of an invisible Church:

> We do not believe in an invisible Church, nor in the kingdom of God existing in the Church as *coetus electorum*; but we believe that God has made the actual empirical Church, in which the Word and the sacraments are administered, into his community, that it is the Body of Christ that is, the presence of Christ in the world, and that according to the promise God's spirit becomes effective in it.[14]

The Church, Bonhoeffer makes clear, is not the result of the will of its members. It is established by God, though he makes himself subject to the will of those who believe.[15]

There is no need to stress how close these themes are to those

[11] Cf. *ibid.*, 163.
[12] *Ibid.*, 148-50.
[13] *Ibid.*, 173-5.
[14] *Ibid.*, 196.
[15] *Ibid.*, 195.

developed in Catholic theologies of the Church. As one would expect, Bonhoeffer is nonetheless anxious at times to make clear the distinctions between his and the Catholic view, in which, it seems to him, the 'historicity [involved in the human condition] is . . . deified as an object',[16] and ultimately 'produces a magical concept of the sacraments'[17] which undermines the absolute authority of the Word of God,[18] sets the institutional Church apart from the community which forms it.[19] . . . We shall never know to what extent his objections would have been done away with by the Constitutions of Vatican II. In any case, he always continued to see in the Catholic Church, as in all Christian bodies, a true *sanctorum communio*. But for him only the evangelical Church was the 'true' Church, chosen by God as 'an especially pure instrument for his work'. It could thus be held to be 'the lap of God's holy Church'.[20]

This concrete and historical concept of the Church was to remain with Bonhoeffer throughout his life. 'The Church is more than prophetic (not less!)', he wrote to a friend in 1932, in reference to the authoritative statements the Church can and must make. 'For it is *Christus praesens*; in the flesh, indeed, in the guise of a human organization, but *Christus praesens* none the less.' The Church is truly 'subject to hearing the command' of God; and he concludes: 'We must not think within an individualistic framework.'[21]

In a group letter he wrote in 1938, entitled: *Our way according to the testimony of Scripture*, he comments upon Ephesians 4:15 ('we are to grow up in every way into him who is the head, into Christ'), a text used at the synod of Dahlem:

> The Church is not a community of souls, as people want to make it today, nor is it simply the proclamation of the Gospel. In other words the Church is not just the pulpit, but the real body of Christ on earth. It is an ordered and well-defined life together which is founded and established by God on this earth. . . . It is

[16] *Ibid.*, 88.
[17] *Ibid.*, 166.
[18] *Ibid.*
[19] *Ibid.*, 177-8.
[20] *Ibid.*, 187.
[21] *G.S.*, I, 64.

a dreadful reduction of the New Testament concept if today the Church is often seen to have its existence only in preaching and the administration of the sacrament. The Church is essentially a gathering round the Word and sacrament; but in addition it is also the whole fullness of gifts, offices and powers which are at work in the community.[22]

In a letter in 1940, he writes in praise of the faith of simple people:

From its first beginnings the Church has belonged to humble, unimportant people. But is it not even today these same people, with pious engravings on their bedrooms walls, who, with overwhelming fidelity, and despite endless opposition, give their pennies for the cause of Christ, support the missionary works in their own communities, and indeed, for love of Jesus Christ, offer their whole lives? . . . It is a fact that it is not educated people, but simple ones, who support the Church; nor does the Gospel give us any reason to wish it otherwise. . . . We shall not for that reason be any the less anxious to be joined by educated people, hoping that they will not be offended by this or that detail, but will come and work together for the building up of the face [of the Church].[23]

In a note on baptism, intended especially to defend the baptism of infants, he spoke again in 1942 against the idea of a Church of the perfect, a Church set apart from the mediocrities of the world:

The nostalgia for a community of believers set apart from the world, a pure and perfect community able to struggle and fight, is very understandable in a Church that has become worldly. But it is very dangerous too. All too easily it opens the way for a [human] ideal of community instead of the real community of God; all too easily does the pure community become seen as a fruit of human effort; all too easily can we forget Jesus's parables about the weeds in the field and the net full of fishes; all too easily can we forget that God loved the *world*, and wants help given to *all mankind*.[24]

A concrete, historical Church must have authority. In 1932,

[22] *G.S.*, II, 327 (*The Way to Freedom*, 178).
[23] *G.S.*, III, 40-1. [24] *G.S.*, III, 450.

at a conference of the World Federation of Youth, Bonhoeffer put the problem of the nature of that authority, and went on to stress the Church's power not only to announce the Gospel, but to give commandments.

> *With whose authority does the Church speak when it declares this claim of Christ to the whole world*? With the authority in which alone the Church can speak, with the authority of the Christ living and present in it. The Church is the presence of Christ on earth, the Church is the *Christus praesens*. For this reason alone its word has authority. The word of the Church is the word of the present Christ, it is gospel and commandment. It would be the retrogression of the Church to the synagogue if its proclamation were commandment alone, and it would be the lapse of the Church into libertinism should it want to deny the commandment of God for the sake of the Gospel.[25]

In a letter to Bethge in 1940, he returns to the experience of the Confessing Church. The battles to be fought and the decisions they involved obviously brought into question the government of the Church, the *Kirchenregiment*, and in doing so made it necessary to reflect on the possibility of an evangelical Church as such:

> We spoke too of the situation of the Church. Once again it became very clear to me in this regard that the struggle over the government of the Church in fact faces us with the question—which must necessarily arise out of the history of the Church—of the possibility of an evangelical Church. The question is to know whether, following the break between papal and secular authority, an authority could be established within the Church based wholly upon the Word and confession of faith. If such an authority should prove to be impossible of attainment, then we have lost our last hope of an evangelical Church. We are left with nothing but either a return to Rome, or submission to the state Church, or otherwise a retreat into individual solitude, the 'protestation' of a real Protestantism against false authorities. It is not by chance, but by divine necessity, that authentic Church government is moving in that direction today.[26]

The problem of Church government is one with the problem of

[25] *G.S.*, I, 144 (*No Rusty Swords*, 161).

[26] *G.S.*, II, 376.

ministries. Bonhoeffer left relatively little written explicitly about this—a few notes only, scattered among the work of his whole career.[27]

For instance, some interesting considerations about ordination and the pastoral ministry can be found in his lecture notes from Finkenwalde. Here Bonhoeffer isolates the 'ministry of preaching', for which one is trained by ordination, from parish ministry which is only one particular and contingent form of the service of the Church. The former, in the Lutheran (as opposed to the Calvinist) view, relates to a mission conferred by the universal Church from which there can be no turning back. Ordination to this ministry, Bonhoeffer notes, seems truly matter for a sacrament. But ordination does not confer the grace of salvation as a sacrament does. In this same context, Bonhoeffer again shows how the inner call to the ministry is normally related to the Church's decision to ordain a man for its services.[28]

On another occasion, he explains how the ministry and the person of the minister are distinct, though interconnected.[29] In *Ethics* he returns in a more general way to the necessity of always maintaining this important distinction between the official function to which a certain power is attached, and the person who exercises it, and of acting accordingly.[30] The function corresponds to a divine order of things which, though imprinted upon human realities, is always greater than the man whose task it is to fulfil it.

When, however, it comes to the Church as we actually know it, a 'pastor' is far more than simply a preacher. Bonhoeffer enlarges on this in a letter to Bethge in 1941 :

> If we are to be 'pastors' of the community, as Christ was, it means something far wider than merely being preachers. . . . The ministry presupposes identification with Christ. That is why it is so noble. Christ was a pastor. We, through him and like him, must be shepherds of men.[31]

[27] Only a few pages of *Sanctorum Communio* are devoted to the point, and there is nothing of any importance in them.

[28] *G.S.*, IV, 248-9.

[29] *G.S.*, IV, 350-51.

[30] *Ethics*, 274.

[31] *G.S.*, II, 412-13.

While it is true to say the ministry exists for the community, the authority that goes with it, as Bonhoeffer points out in *Ethics*, is not thereby ultimately based upon that community. It comes not from below, but from above.

> The spiritual office is the divinely ordained authority to exercise spiritual dominion by divine right. It does not proceed from the congregation but from God.[32]

It is a ministry that concerns not only discipline, but doctrine as well: the doctrine which, as Luther put it, is of 'heaven', where life is of 'earth'. Or, rather, the discipline which governs the life of the community is primarily based upon a discipline relating to doctrine. From this point of view, Bonhoeffer has no objection to the idea of a 'magisterium'.[33] He speaks of this particularly in *The Cost of Discipleship*[34] and the *Ethics*:

> Holy Scripture belongs essentially to the office of teaching. If indivdiual Christians or a group of Christians seize hold of the Bible, appealing to the equal right of all Christians, to the right of the faithful to speak for themselves, and to the self-evident truth of the scriptural word, it is by no means a sign of special reverence or special spiritual understanding for the essential character of the divine revelation.[35]

Bonhoeffer was not just repeating an empty formula when he declared that the Christian faith lives only in the Church.

Theology as the knowledge of the Church

In Bonhoeffer's mind, his qualifying thesis for higher education which he defended in 1931 under the title *Akt und Sein (Act and Being)*, was to complete *Sanctorum Communio*, by going more deeply into the fundamental philosophico-theological problems involved in the Church's teaching. Or rather, he intended to show in it how it is only by rightly understanding the reality of the

[32] *Ethics*, 333. The complementary view is developed further in *Sanctorum Communion*, 161ff.
[33] In German *Lehramt*.
[34] *The Cost of Discipleship*, 264-5.
[35] *Ethics*, 295.

Church that we will find the solution to the major problems of philosophy and theology.

The philosophy and theology of the day seemed to Bonhoeffer to be split in two ways: in philosophy between the Kantian stream of transcendental critique and the ontology brought back into current thinking by Martin Heidegger; in theology between the actualism of Karl Barth and several representatives of 'dialectical theology', and the ontology of classical theology, freshly interpreted in modern terms by Erich Przywara. Though these problems are far from having been solved, and indeed have rarely been considered since his time at the same depth—at least by theologians—I shall only briefly recall Bonhoeffer's somewhat technical argument.

> Inasmuch as analysis of revelation in terms whether of act or being produces concepts of knowledge unsuited to bear the whole weight of revelation, the idea of revelation must be envisaged within the concretion of the idea of the Church, i.e. in a sociological category where both kinds of analysis encounter each other and are drawn together in one. The dialectic of act and being is here recognizable in theological terms as the dialectic of faith and the communion of Christ; neither is to be imagined without the other, but each 'suspended' in the other.[36]

Thus, in the whole book, Bonhoeffer's purpose is to harmonize the actualist with the ontological point of view.

> The whole represents an attempt to unify the aims of true transcendentalism and true ontology within an 'ecclesiastical thought'.[37]

After a chapter on philosophy, Bonhoeffer goes on first to expound and then to criticize the interpretation of Revelation in actualist terms, and also its interpretation in ontological terms. He shows in particular how the purely actualist concept of Revelation corresponds to a formal notion of the sovereign liberty of God—a liberty that has been, and will always be, manifested in the *gift* of the Word and the Covenant. 'God *is there* . . . "haveable" graspable in his Word within the Church.'[38] And it is an

[36] *Act and Being*, 15-16.
[37] *Ibid.*, 16.
[38] *Ibid.*, 90-91.

abstraction to see the Word as simply spoken to the individual. Man is never a 'single unit', nor can he be addressed in the singular, but 'invariably finds himself in some community, whether "in Adam" or "in Christ".' We can thus say that 'the being of Revelation "is" the being of a community of persons constituted and embraced by the person of Christ, wherein the individual finds himself to be already in his new existence'.[39]

It seems that statements of this kind could well be a fairly decisive critique of Protestant theology. Yet here again Bonhoeffer indicates how far he is from Catholic ideas, as he understands them, especially those relating to what he calls 'the institutional Catholic Church'.[40] He makes it clear, in fact, that we must distinguish (which Catholicism certainly does not seem to him to do adequately) between the 'is' used of persons and the 'there is' used of things.[41] It is clearly only the personalist and community point of view which makes it possible to explain Revelation and all the realities it creates and expresses. This conviction led Bonhoeffer to conclude his study by analysing 'being' in Adam and 'being' in Christ.

But what seems to me the most important thing to note is the purpose of the project for which this small, carefully worked-out book was written. The author wanted to put into it a kind of treatise on 'the knowledge of faith', or 'theological knowledge', a treatise in which theology is conceived and presented not so much purely and simply in terms of 'existential knowledge', as in terms of 'ecclesial knowledge':[42]

> Theology is a function of the Church, for Church there is none without preaching, nor preaching without remembrance, but theology is the memory of the Church. As such it assists the Church to understand the premises of Christian preaching, helps it, in other words, to form dogmas.[43]

In the inaugural lecture he gave in 1930 in the aula of the

[39] *Ibid.*, 122-3. [40] *Ibid.*, 123.
[41] *Ibid.*, 125. The translator adds a footnote: 'It may be worth remarking that the German *es gibt* is more firmly linked than "there is" with notions of "the given", the available, hence dominable, manipulable'.
[42] Cf. *ibid.*, 137, 143ff. [43] *Ibid.*, 143.

university of Berlin, on 'Man in contemporary philosophy and theology', he was already stressing the essentially ecclesial nature of true theological thinking. He concluded his lecture with these words:

> Only as the thought of the Church does theological thought in the last resort remain the only thought which does not rationalize reality by the category of possibility. Thus not only does every individual theological problem point back to the reality of the Church of Christ, but theological thought recognizes itself in its totality as something which belongs alone to the Church.[44]

Again, it was while teaching at the university of Berlin, in 1933, that he showed the requirements for, and the importance of, the vocation of the true theologian needed by the Church. Here quality was more important than quantity. And it would certainly not be right to take up theological studies simply because one could not qualify properly for any others. But nor must the motive be a more or less subjective inner experience of a 'vocation'; rather one must feel drawn by the subject to be studied:

> [The future theologian] must not think he has to wait for certain recognizable experiences indicating that he has a 'vocation'. No, he must recognize a vocation to theology in the fact of being gripped by its subject matter and unable to leave it alone. But, of course, it must be the genuine object of theology he is concerned with; in other words, he must be disposed to think about God, his Word, and his will, and to meditate 'on his law day and night' (Ps 1:2). . . . It is not a sense of calling, but an aptitude for sober, serious, responsible theological work, which must be the starting point for theological studies.[45]

The candidate for theological studies, and the ministry for which they are the preparation must, he continues, be 'a full man', open to all genuine human passions and understanding.

> But as a theologian, he must at the same time, learn and know that the mainspring of his life and thought as a theologian can only depend on the passion of Jesus Christ, the crucified Lord.[46]

[44] *G.S.*, III, 84 (*No Rusty Swords*, 69).
[45] *G.S.*, II, 243. [46] *G.S.*, III, 244.

It is not in the smothering of human vitality, but in the encounter of the cross as the goal of every problem, every search, that there is effected that conversion without which no one can attain to the true object of theology.

The theology student need not feel ashamed of the subject matter of his study, or try to escape from it. He certainly need not blush to be in 'company with true theologians, from Paul to Luther, via Augustine and Thomas', nor to be seeking the answer to questions 'which appear vital to the most serious and clear-sighted of men'. Nor need he try to play the man of the world; this would do nothing for his prestige, but only harm him. He must, on the contrary, take his place in the Church, humbly but earnestly. He must be ready to 'discern spirits', not 'to whitewash what is black, but to call truth truth and error error'. And the touchstone of this is his knowledge of the authentic mind of the Church.[47]

> He must know where to find the source of the Church's life, and how it can be dried up or poisoned. He must learn to recognize where and when Christ's Church stands at the moment of decision, the moment when he must confess his faith in a *status confessionis*.[48]

If genuine theological knowledge is 'ecclesial knowledge', bound up with the actual life of the Church, it is because the being and action of that Church always exceed its conscious knowledge. This idea recurs several times in Bonhoeffer's writings and is one of his firmest convictions. 'Theology and the question of the Church', he wrote in a communal letter in 1936, 'stem from the empirical experiences of the Church in her encounters.'[49]

That is why creed and dogma are not synonymous with theology. Whereas the latter is of the nature of systematic speculation, creeds and dogmas are essentially related to life. Bonhoeffer stresses this point most strongly in a study of the unity of the Church—to which I shall be returning later:

> The confession is the Church's decision about its boundaries, made

[47] *G.S.*, III, 245-6. [48] *G.S.*, III, 246.
[49] *G.S.*, III, 325-6 (*The Way to Freedom*, 43).

on the basis of theology. It is not a representation of the whole of the Church's teaching, but a decision of the Church taken on the basis of the whole of its teaching to join the battle at a specific place. . . . Orthodoxy confuses confession with a theological system. The confessionless confuse the Church's confession with the testimony of piety.[50]

The Church's teaching, in other words, is inseparable from its actual life, from its living awareness of itself and its mission. It is neither a purely intellectual gnosis, nor the mere expression of pious sentiments, but the declaration of a faith which must be conceptually accountable, but which comes primarily from its unbreakable bond with Jesus Christ and the living Word which forms it. Thus, Bonhoeffer explains, in another communal letter, dated Christmas 1939, the early Church was able to confess Christ truly in obedience, labour and struggle, and we can always deepen our own faith by going back to that:

The early Church reflected for several centuries on the problem of Christ. In considering it, she combined reasoning with obedience to Jesus Christ, and in difficult and often paradoxical formulæ has provided us with a living witness to the mystery of his person. She did not succumb to the modern illusion that we can only know that mystery through emotion or inner experience; for she knew how introverted and easily corrupted all inner experience and human sentiment can be. She did not, of course, think that the mystery could be plumbed any better by logic; but, while boldly formulating the ultimate conceptual paradoxes, she made a point of witnessing and glorifying the mystery precisely as a mystery to any natural thinking. The Christology of the early Church originated in the stable in Bethlehem, and the splendour of Christmas shines again in her face. Even today it still delights the heart of whoever learns to know it. . . . The hard ideas of that time are like flints from which to strike fire.[51]

His concrete sense of the Church forced Bonhoeffer, if not to develop a theory of tradition, at least to stress the need for being ready to learn from it, and above all, to try to gain a real understanding of the Bible. Sometime between 1936 and 1939 he wrote:

[50] *G.S.*, II, 227, 235 (*ibid.*, 83, 91).

[51] *G.S.*, III, 383.

> From that book the Church has been drawing her knowledge of the truth for two thousand years. We are not the first to read it attentively. Liberal theology has not always had the humility to recognize this fact. The Reformation and the early Church are more important interpreters than we are.[52]

And he wrote again from prison, in a letter dated November 1943:

> I am now reading Tertullian, Cyprian, and others of the Church Fathers with great interest. In some ways they are more relevant to our times than the Reformers, and at the same time they provide a basis for talks between Protestants and Roman Catholics.[53]

For him, theology was always a working out of his faith, the fulfilment of a mission. Thus, when in the heat of the battle, in February 1941, he wondered what he would do if he knew he had only four or six months more to live, he was able to write: 'I think I should still try to teach theology as I have always done, and to preach often.'[54]

The frontiers of the Church and the need for truth

If the Church is a concrete, historical reality, she must necessarily consider the problem of her frontiers. The theological positions taken up by Bonhoeffer at the time of *Sanctorum Communio* inevitably led him to study the question. But it also arose unavoidably out of the situation created by the formation of the Confessing Church and its confrontation with the German Christians. It was essential to be able to recognize the true Church, to distinguish it from its sacrilegious counterfeits, and to define who were its legitimate representatives, who its members, and at what point divergences or hesitations became unacceptable. To Bonhoeffer, the problem appeared not only within the German Church but, as I said earlier, in relation to problems posed by the ecumenical movement. What could that movement mean if those

[52] *G.S.*, IV, 255-6.
[53] *Letters and Papers from Prison*, 97.
[54] *G.S.*, II, 405.

who had betrayed Christianity were represented in it alongside those who practised authentic Christianity? In other words, could the movement simply disregard the fundamental question of truth? And Bonhoeffer, though people sometimes try today to make him the hero of ultra-liberalism, was in fact an impassioned defender of truth and its irreducible demands.

The problem of the frontiers of the Church and its unity was discussed by him in a lecture in 1936, later published in the review *Evangelische Theologie*, on 'Church Union'.[55]

In it he explains that the Reformation was very concerned to point out where the Church was to be found: wherever the gospel was truly proclaimed and the sacraments rightly administered. It had no intention of establishing that Church's boundaries, which could be known only to God. The believer had only, thankfully, to recognize the Church of God where it *was*, where it brought him salvation. 'Why should he ask where it is not, if he is completely swallowed up in that joy?'[56] The manifestation of the Church was one with the proclamation of the Good News of salvation. To be concerned over boundaries would be to see it not in the light of the Gospel, but only of the Law.

Yet the Church is subjected to resistance from unbelief. And, in a sense, its boundaries are revealed by what it is not. That is why it cannot arrange or define them *a priori* in any theoretical way. To think that it could seemed to Bonhoeffer an illusion resulting from a misunderstanding of the Church's nature, an illusion to be found both in Protestant orthodoxy and in Pietism (two extremes which modern Protestantism is continually having to steer between), and also in Catholicism, in which he appears not to see the link between teaching and living witness. The fact is that, in a concept of the Church arising out of the Reformation, the determining of its frontiers implies 'the moment of living decision'.

> Therefore the question of Church membership can only be answered concretely in the authoritative decision of the Church.

[55] *G.S.*, II, 217ff. (*The Way to Freedom*, 75-96).
[56] *G.S.*, II, 218 (*ibid.*, 76).

> This characteristic of decision is a purely objective one. It would be both subjective and arbitrary were the Church to wish to draw the boundaries beforehand and thus to complete the division of its own accord. The apparent objectivity of a theoretical knowledge of the boundaries of the Church is itself a dissolution of the true objectivity which is achieved in decision.[57]

To make those decisions, however, the Church does possess certain criteria, even though they may only emerge out of the actual movement of her history. Thus she first of all came to recognize baptism as a basic factor in forming her frontiers. But this was not adequate of itself, for there could be heretics who were baptized, dead members, and conversely, genuine witnesses to the faith who had not yet been baptized. The Church came to understand that with baptism there must be linked the confession of faith. But what would be a necessary and sufficient confession of faith to define the ecclesial community? The answer to this question was an 'act, a decision of the Church, which could never be formulated in terms of logical or theological requirements'. For the unity of the Church never results merely from putting together all that we hold in common and seeing it to be quantitatively greater than our differences. It is a 'qualitative totality', and a single point of difference could be enough to destroy it. That is why 'it cannot be produced by comparison; it must be given unity'.[58]

Since the frontiers of the Church are revealed to her by the experience of collision with all that is not herself, their definition will vary in the light of circumstances. 'It may well be that a situation which is dangerous today is no longer decisive for the course of the war tomorrow', just as a mere difference of opinion may one day be seen as able to destroy the unity of the Church.[59]

Indeed what happened in the case of the German Christians was a lesson that correct doctrinal formulae may actually become an instrument of heresy—for the fact is that truth is only to be found in that concrete totality which is the true Church.

[57] *G.S.*, II, 222 (*ibid.*, 70).
[58] *G.S.*, II, 224-5 (*ibid.*, 82).
[59] *G.S.*, II, 225-6 (*ibid.*, 82-3).

> Right teaching becomes false teaching the moment it is used in the struggle against the true Church. To continue the figure of a war: in such an instance the officers desert with their weapons and their men go over to the enemy camp. They have the same weapons as the army they have betrayed, but they are now directing them against their former friends.[60]

It is important here, however, to make a clear distinction between a 'false Church', the Church of Antichrist, and an 'erring Church': with this latter there can be dialogue leading to wider mutual understanding, but with the former only a fight to the death. In neither case however must the Church shirk her duty of making her frontiers absolutely clear. Even if doing so is a task that seems to it 'strange' to its own inner life, it is ultimately 'a merciful act both to its members and to those outside. It is the last, the "strange", possibility of making the call to salvation audible.'[61]

After having set out these general considerations, Bonhoeffer goes on in the same lecture to look at the problems actually presented to the Church by the German Christians. For one could not think them wholly solved by the statements of Barmen and Dahlem. The Church still had to decide upon her attitude towards the parishes and parish councils of those who wanted to remain 'neutral'. This involved on her part a fresh existential act, an authoritative decision to be made in obedience to the Word of God. She could not rest content with drawing purely logical conclusions from the formulae fixed by the synods, nor with simply recalling the basic attitude they defined.

> The Church will recognize friend or enemy by the confession, but the confession is not an ultimate, clear-cut measure. The Church must decide where the enemy is standing.[62]

And, as we have seen, in the battle she was forced into, all the old lines of demarcation had naturally shifted. Thus members of the Reformed Church and Lutherans could find themselves together in the same Confessing Church. This unusual phenomenon —which can only be accounted for by the great power of the

[60] *G.S.*, II, 228 (*ibid.*, 84-5).
[61] *G.S.*, II, 229 (*ibid.*, 85-6).
[62] *G.S.*, II, 235 (*ibid.*, 91).

gospel—is incomprehensible to the 'orthodox' believer who confounds faith with the terminology in which it is expressed, just as it is to the liberal or the pietist for whom *any* firmness in holding to a defined faith must mean being closed to the ever-new impulses of the Spirit:

> The orthodox does not understand how it can be possible to treat the clauses of the confession in a different way. He does not understand the openness of the Lutherans of the Confessing Church towards the Reformed or towards the ecumenical movement. Those without a confession, among the great number of pastors under the sway of Pietism and liberal theology, do not, on the other hand, understand the obstinacy in the application of the doctrinal concept against the German Christians.[63]

The third section of the lecture draws some very definite conclusions, which it would certainly be hard to fit in with the simplified, and sometimes even distorted, idea so many people have of Bonhoeffer's message:

> *Extra ecclesiam nulla salus.* The question of Church membership is the question of salvation. The boundaries of the Church are the boundaries of salvation. Whoever knowingly cuts himself off from the Confessing Church in Germany cuts himself off from salvation.[64]

Bonhoeffer knew that in saying such things he was in effect suporting one of the basic tenets of Catholicism. Yet in itself this fact did not alarm him. What was necessary was to understand this traditional teaching of Christianity correctly.

> Is that not the Roman heresy of the Church? In so far as Roman doctrine cannot think of salvation without the Church and cannot think of the Church without salvation, it is right. But in so far as the statement that there is only salvation in the Church means anything but the call to the visible Church, in so far then as this statement is not an existential expression of the faith of the true Church but is intended as a theoretical truth about the saved and the lost, in so far as it is anything but an offer of grace, the means of salvation, it is reprehensible. For then a statement of faith is a

[63] *G.S.*, II, 235 (*ibid.*, 90). [64] *G.S.*, II, 238 (*ibid.*, 93-4).

speculative statement. *Extra ecclesiam nulla salus* is in the strict sense a statement of faith.[65]

In all this the same conviction remains clear: it is impossible to talk about the Church independently of the commitment of faith. This is not, however, to say that the mystery of the Church is not far richer than anything faith can say about it, just as the true God is everywhere, though for us he is not to be sought, outside his revelation.[66]

But it is the Church's mission, as Bonhoeffer says repeatedly, which obliges her to mark her frontiers clearly, and thus bear witness to saving truth.

> It must be said again and again that for the Church to deny its boundaries is no work of mercy. The true Church comes up against boundaries. In recognizing them it does the work of love towards men by honouring the truth.[67]

Bonhoeffer remained intransigent to the end on the question of truth. Not only did he make this clear with the utmost rigidity in his refusal to compromise in any way with the German Christians; he kept it in the forefront in all his ecumenical work; he refused to acept the 'branch' theory so popular at the time, which considered the different Churches or confessions as forming the branches of a single Church, which could contain them all without being identified with any one of them. 'Yet this is the construction which the Confessing Church must destroy' because of its exclusive claims as the evangelical Church in Germany. The branch theory really only served to obscure the seriousness of the ecumenical problem, and that of the Church as a whole.[68] To Bonhoeffer the notion of 'heresy' was as absolutely indispensable

[65] *G.S.*, II, 239 (*ibid.*, 94).

[66] *G.S.*, II, 241 (*ibid.*, 96). In effect, says Bonhoeffer in a letter written at the same period, 'the significance of excommunication must be seen in relation to our knowledge of the judgment and the separation effected by God at the end'. For the rest, the Church's object is not so much to effect a judgment as to preach the Gospel, and by preaching it to lead people to divide of themselves (*G.S.*, II, 243-4).

[67] *G.S.*, II, 240 (*ibid.*, 95).

[68] *G.S.*, I, 251 (*No Rusty Swords*, 335-6).

to the Church and to the way of life of the faithful as was ecclesiastical discipline.[69]

Reflecting upon his experience of American Christian life in his 1939 report, entitled *Protestantism without Reformation*, he refers to the undoubtedly attractive idea that the pragmatism of American Christianity might provide a satisfactory basis for Church unity. But, he says, it is in fact the reverse that is true:

> Where no struggle for truth divides the Churches, the unity of the Church should already have been won. The actual picture, however, is just the opposite. Precisely here, where the question of truth is not the criterion of Church communion and Church division, disintegration is greater than anywhere else.[70]

It is in its commitment to truth that the Church finds its unity. It was because Christianity in America had never had to make the kind of decisions made during the Reformation that it presented a spectacle of such endless divisions.[71]

As regards Catholicism, he considered that Asmussen, who preached during a service organized by the *Una Sancta* movement, went 'too far', 'was wholly inconsistent'.[72] Not that he himself rejected unity with the Catholic Church out of hand, or despaired of ever achieving it: but he considered that, like the unity reached by the Reformed and Lutheran Churches in the *Kirchenkampf*, it could only be brought about through the 'recognition of God's "guidance" ' of their destiny in the world, and also that of 'the objectivity of Christ's presence'—in other words by way of a new kind of act of faith.

In his memoir, the Lutheran bishop Gerhard Jacobi speaks forcefully of Bonhoeffer's firmness of faith:

> Dietrich Bonhoeffer never for a moment doubted in the trinitarian God. He would have fought to the death against our modern flirting with unbelief.[73]

[69] Cf. *G.S.*, I, 126, 127 (*No Rusty Swords*, 173-82), 180; II, 236 (*The Way to Freedom*, 91); IV, 335; *The Cost of Discipleship*, 264-5.
[70] *G.S.*, I, 328 (*No Rusty Swords*, 96). [71] *G.S.*, I, 328-9 (*ibid.*, 96-7).
[72] *G.S.*, II, 380. [73] *Begegnung mit Bonhoeffer*, 56.

Pastor Albrecht Schönherr tells a story which underlines this, In the early days of the *Kirchenkampf*, Bonhoeffer heard of a pastor who had the idea of entering the German Christian movement in order to try to influence it from within. This plan, though thoroughly well-intentioned, made him literally rush into action. He went without more ado to the man concerned and said: 'If I get into the wrong train, it is no use running along the corridor in the opposite direction to the way it is going.'[74]

Bonhoeffer was never a dreamer in his conception of the Church, any more than in the concrete attitudes he wanted to see in its members.

The Church and the world

Bonhoeffer's concrete, incarnate, historic sense of the Church never led him, however, at any time, to think of it as self sufficient. Its stability it owed to God, and it existed only in its mission. The truth to which it was bound, and which made any compromise with error impossible, was its 'weapon' in its unending life-and-death struggle. Yet 'with this truth it knows itself to be called not to rule, but to serve and to listen'.[75] Having, as we have seen,[76] stressed its special inwardness by his statement that it had a certain 'inner finality', he became more and more insistent upon its mission to the world, to such a point that he seems almost to be contradicting himself in his condemnation of the temptation of making itself 'an end in itself'.[77] As well as his knowledge of the importance of the subject, circumstances continually arose which led

[74] *Ibid.*, 101.

[75] *G.S.*, I, 260 (*No Rusty Swords*, 343). Here he is referring explicitly to the Confessing Church. But, as we know, this was for Bonhoeffer the exemplar of the true Church.

[76] Cf. *supra*, p. 41.

[77] Cf. *Letters and Papers from Prison*, 160. In the *Ethics*, Bonhoeffer shows how the Church is both means and end. He sees Catholicism as being in danger of making the Church too exclusively its own end, whereas Protestantism is more likely to forget that God wills the Church to exist at all. He himself considers that the idea of 'deputyship' or 'mandate' is the most helpful in enabling us to grasp these two aspects of the Church and their relationship to one another (*Ethics*, 301-2).

him to explain just how he conceived this relationship between the Church and the world, or, from a slightly different standpoint, the relationship between faith and everyday life.

One of his most telling developments of the point comes in a lecture he gave in 1932 under the title *Dein Reich komme*! (Thy Kingdom Come). In it he takes special pains to point out the danger of the Church turning in upon itself, alienating itself in an attempt to compensate for a lack of vitality, and the opposite, though similar, danger of identifying its mission with the work of this world, mere secularization disguised as the service of God.

> We are the inhabitants of an other-world, or else we are totally secularized men; that is to say, we no longer believe in the kingdom of God. We are enemies of the world, because we want to be better than it is, or else we are enemies of God, because he is taking our mother the earth away from us. We flee from the power of the world, or else we cling to it. But we are not travellers who love the world that bears us along, but who love it truly only because they are travelling across it towards another world which they love above everything else—for otherwise they would not be travelling in the first place. You can only believe in the Kingdom of God if you are such a traveller, if you love both the world and God.
>
> We are the inhabitants of an other-world, for we have discovered a cheating trick of being religious and even 'Christian', at the world's expense. In an other-worldly existence one can live splendidly. As soon as life begins to be painful or inconvenient, we make a bold leap into the air and arrive, rested and carefree, in what we call eternal dwelling.[78]

There are no lack of reasons given to justify this kind of turning inwards. After all, the Church must be merciful and compassionate to the weak; she must keep them a refuge in the other world. Here Bonhoeffer's answer is in no uncertain terms:

> The weak man must be helped. He is helped by Christ. Yet Christ does not will his weakness, but makes him strong. He does not lead him into the other-world of a religious flight from the world, but gives him back to the earth as its faithful son. Do not be inhabitants of an other-world, but be strong![79]

Are only power, energy and action, then, to be praised? The

[78] *G.S.*, III, 270-1. [79] *G.S.*, III, 271.

other world as an escape is not the only way of caricaturing the Kingdom of God. We can also caricature it by setting out to build up that Kingdom by our own efforts, trying to give it a worldly grandeur alongside other kingdoms. And because to do so is to create an *other* world, *alongside* the real world, this caricature is not basically very different from the first.

> [We are inhabitants of an other-world]. . . . Or else we are the children of this world. . . . We have succumbed to the spirit of the age; even if it is the pious spirit of the age, the Christian spirit of the age. . . . We must represent God's business. We must build for ourselves a solid fortress in which we can live with God in safety. We build the Kingdom. Or one can live just as splendidly with the optimistic spirit of the age. Man—religious man included—finds delight in struggling and in displaying his strength. . . .[80]

And here too there is no lack of noble motives. After all, surely it is right for the Church to have under its banner the brave, the determined, the faithful children of the world, in order to be able to carry on its holy war? Yet the God we claim to serve in this way is turned into an idol by our claim :

> To escape from God himself while declaring ourselves ready to re-establish his rule in the world, to love the world for itself, for that battle [which we fight in it] : that is simply our Christian fashion of succumbing to the spirit of secularism. Yet we cannot escape from God. He takes man under his rule again. Become weak in the world, and let God be the Lord ![81]

And Bonhoeffer shows that the underlying principle common to both attitudes is simply one of unbelief.

> Existing in another world and sharing in the spirit of the age are but two faces of the same reality : *not believing in the Kingdom of God*. The man who flees from the world to escape its suffering does not believe; but neither does the man who thinks he has himself to build up God's Kingdom like a kingdom in the world. The man who escapes from the world does not find God, but simply another world, his own world, better, more beautiful, more peaceful, an other-world; he never finds God's world, for that comes into this world. The man who escapes from the world to find God finds only himself. The man who escapes from God to

[80] *G.S.*, III, 271-2. [81] *G.S.*, III, 272-3.

find the world does not find the world as God's world; he finds it an amusing drama of the war between good and evil, between religion and irreligion, a war of which he is himself the cause; he finds only himself.[82]

The Kingdom of God comes on earth, an earth overgrown with brambles and thorns, through his grace. It is sought for in prayer —the prayer of those who, even in the midst of the world, have recognized the good news and its force for resurrection.

Thy Kingdom come! That is a prayer which the pious soul of the person who flees from the world cannot say; nor can the Utopian, the fanatic, the impassioned reformer. It can only be the prayer of the children of the world, who do not set themselves apart, who have no miraculous recipes for making everything better, who are not superior to the world, but in its midst, in the daily round, are deeply subject to it, persevering together because it is precisely by doing so that they are faithful to life, and fixing their gaze on that one place in the world where they are struck with wonder to see the lifting of the curse, the profound assent given by God to the world's plea: that one place where, in the midst of this dying, broken, thirsting world, the resurrection of Christ can be seen by whoever can believe in it. . . . The Kingdom of God is the *Kingdom of the Resurrection* on earth.[83]

The coming of the Kingdom of God must be seen in no other terms than the coming of God himself as we know him by revelation. For 'where God is, there is his Kingdom':

How will the Kingdom of God come to us? No differently from God himself; in the destruction of the law of death, in the resurrection, in miracle, and yet, at the same time, in the affirmation of the world, in an entry into its own order, its communities, its history. The two are interlinked. For it is only where the world is wholly accepted that it can be truly broken and destroyed; and only the lifting of the curse on the earth makes it possible to take that earth really seriously.[84]

Thus, like God himself, his Kingdom always comes to us 'in a twofold form': in the form of 'miracle', which triumphs over the subjection to vanity and death that characterizes all the kingdoms

[82] *G.S.*, III, 273.
[83] *G.S.*, III, 276.
[84] *G.S.*, III, 278.

and works of this world, and in the form of 'order' which enables the world to remain in existence. This double form under which the Kingdom of God comes on earth is, in the concrete, partly the Church and partly the State.

> Miracle and order—these are the two forms under which the Kingdom of God appears on earth, the two forms of its twofold and distinct manifestation. Miracle, as a breaking of all our orders, and order as the support of what is ordered to the miraculous. But miracle is also surrounded by the world of order, and order keeps itself complete, in its limitations, through miracle. The form in which the Kingdom of God appears as miracle we call the Church; the form in which it appears as order we call the State.[85]

Church and State mutually limit one another on the 'stage' of the *People*, for whom both are realities, and to both of which they owe obedience, since these are the two essential modalities of the coming of the Kingdom of God.

However, notes Bonhoeffer in conclusion, those two modalities remain provisional in nature, just as the figure of this world which shall pass away is provisional, whereas the Kingdom of God is for eternity. Nevertheless, its fulfilment will be achieved in the creation of a new heaven and a new *earth*—but a really *new* earth, in which all barriers will be removed.

> And there will no longer be Church or State, but both will hand back their responsibility to him from whom they received it first.[86]

Bonhoeffer comes back several times to this reciprocal relationship between Church and State, which represents the two facets of God's action in the world. Thus in an article in that same year, 1932, entitled 'What is the Church?', he wrote:

> In proclaiming the commandment and the grace of God, the Church stands at the limit, at the limit of human possibilities, which has been penetrated from above. But, in that it speaks of the penetration of the limit, of the laws of the world, while standing itself as a human institution completely within this limit, it points to these laws, these orders of the world, to whose annihilation, destruction and ending through God, it so powerfully testifies.

[85] *G.S.*, III, 279. Cf. *Ethics*, 60-62.

[86] *G.S.*, III, 283.

> The preaching of the Church is therefore necessarily 'political', i.e. it is directed at the order of politics in which man is engaged. But precisely because it is 'political' it is primarily concerned with the critical limit of all political action. The Church is the limit of politics and therefore eminently political and a-political at the same time. Because the Church testifies to the penetration of the limit, it points to the limit, to the law, to order, to the State. The Church limits the State, the State limits the Church.[87]

Thus Bonhoeffer did not by any means visualize a system of absolute separation between Church and State as the ideal. He was even more sure of this after experiencing the American situation. In the diary he made of the journey, he noted in 1939:

> I find it more and more difficult to understand how the principle of a separation of Church and State fits in with the practice of the social, economic, organizational and political activity of the Church. In any case, the separation of Church and State does not result in the Church continuing to apply itself to its own task; it is no guarantee against secularization. Nowhere is the Church more secularized than where it is separated in principle as it is here. This very separation can create an opposition, so that the Church engages much more strongly in political and secular things.[88]

He always spoke out against those *simpliste* solutions which consist merely in juxtaposing the temporal and the spiritual, or, conversely, in mixing them together. They could only, it seemed to him, exist in reference to each other, mutually supporting each other. He says this again in *Ethics*:

> Luther was protesting against a Christianity which was striving for independence and detaching itself from the reality in Christ. He protested with the help of the secular and in the name of a better Christianity. So, too, today, when Christianity is employed as a polemical weapon against the secular, this must be done in the name of a better secularity, and above all it must not lead back to a static predominance of the spiritual sphere as an end in itself.[89]

Of course the Church must always have its own space. It must

[87] *G.S.*, III, 289 (*No Rusty Swords*, 156).
[88] *G.S.*, I, 311 (*The Way to Freedom*, 239).
[89] *Ethics*, 199.

never be reduced to a 'purely spiritual force'. But its own being only keeps its true significance in relation to the being of the world, just as the world only finds its laws of life in relation to the Church. Church and world do not coincide, but rather respond to their true destiny by continually passing into one another.

> The space of the Church is not there in order to try to deprive the world of a piece of its territory, but precisely in order to prove to the world that it is still the world, the world which is loved by God and reconciled with him.[90]

Christ, the centre of all things

The reconciling of God and the world is effected in Jesus Christ. There is no ecclesiology without Christology. The Church as 'Christus praesens' was one of the most important themes in *Sanctorum Communio*. 'Christ existing as a Church'—this is another phrase we find running through the book. Yet Bonhoeffer has left us no study of Christology as systematic or developed as his studies of ecclesiology. The most important consists in a course he gave in Berlin in 1933, but it has only been able to be reconstructed from notes made by his students.[91]

One of the *leitmotivs* of this fragmentary work is that to Jesus Christ our question should not be 'How?', but 'Who?' Here is yet another application of the idea of theological knowledge as an existential knowledge, a knowledge of faith. ' "How are you possible?"—that is *the* godless question, the serpent's question'; whereas, ' "Who are you?" is *the* religious question.' It is the Church's question, and only with the Church can an authentic Christology be constructed.[92]

Our Christology must be none the less scientific for that:

[90] *Ethics*, 202. One whole section of the *Ethics*, which I have already had occasion to quote from, but which was never completed, is devoted to the question of 'State and Church' (332 ff.).

[91] *G.S.*, III, 166 ff. This was also published separately under the title *Wer ist und wer war Jesus Christus? Seine Geschichte und sein Geheimnis* (Hamburg, 1962), and in English as *Christology* (London, 1966). It is to this latter that the page numbers given here will refer.

[92] *Christology*, 30-31.

Bonhoeffer was never content with the pietist position. But the task of a scientific Christology, if it is not to fail of its true object, 'is to work out the ontological structure of the "Who", without coming to grief on the Scylla of the question "How?" or the Charybdis of the "fact" of revelation.'[93] His Christology is thus very sharply distinguished from that of, say, Bultmann, to whom the whole mystery of Jesus is to be summed up precisely in the simple 'fact that' *(Dass)* he exists; and for him, to want to give it any other content than that would be the result of 'objectivizing thought', which would lead us unavoidably to the 'elements of this world' with which faith as such can have no dealings. Bonhoeffer also refused to follow Bultmann in merging Christology with soteriology. To reduce Christology to soteriology was, he explained, the intention of Melanchthon, whose formula on the subject we know so well: *'Hoc est Christum cognoscere, beneficia ejus cognoscere'*[94] (to know Christ is to know the good he has done for us). 'This', he adds, 'was an epoch-making view. It was carried on by Schleiermacher and Ritschl.' But for Luther, on the other hand, 'the person interprets the work'.[95]

> So there is no access to the work except through the person. . . . Whether his work perishes in the world of death or whether it abides in a new world of life depends upon the person of Christ.[96]

Not, of course, that one must therefore separate the person from the work.

> The Christological question, of its very nature, must be addressed to the whole Christ, the one Christ. The whole Christ is the historical *(geschichtliche)* Jesus who can never in any way be divorced from his work. He is asked and he replies as the one who is himself his work. But Christology primarily seeks his being and not his action. To put it in abstract terms: the subject of Christology is the personal structure of being of the whole, historical Jesus Christ.[97]

Just as Christology cannot be reduced to soteriology, so neither

[93] *Ibid.*, 33.
[94] *Ibid.*, 37-8.
[95] *Ibid.*, 38.
[96] *Ibid.*, 38-9.
[97] *Ibid.*, 40.

can once, again as Bultmann does, be content to see Jesus Christ as simply a bearer of the Word of God :

> In that case the important thing would not be his person, but his mission. But the New Testament contradicts this understanding.[98]

Christ is the Word of God 'as the Son'. He is Word, but he is sacrament as well, and 'the sacrament is distinct from the Word and has a specific justification for its existence', relating to the body.[99]

And finally, Christ is also Community. That Community '*is* the body of Christ'. 'He is not only the head of the community, but also the community itself.' (Cf. 1 Cor 12 and Ephesians.)[100]

Bonhoeffer's determinedly theological and ecclesial standpoint led him to start from a consideration of Christ as living, as present. But he was equally certain that that living, contemporary Christ was none other than the historical Jesus who was born in Nazareth and died on the cross. Though remaining distinct, the historical point of view and the point of view of faith were for him inseparably linked.

> We have so far spoken of the present Christ; but this present-historical *(geschichtlich)* Christ is the same person as the historical *(historisch)* Jesus of Nazareth. Were this not so, we would have to say with Paul that our faith is vain and an illusion. The Church would be deprived of its substance. There can be no isolation of the so-called historical *(historisch)* Jesus from the Christ who is present now. . . . The historicity *(Geschichtlichkeit)* of Jesus Christ thus comes under the twofold aspect of history *(Historie)* and faith. Both aspects are closely associated.[101]

Since any valid Christology must always develop within the faith of the Church, Bonhoeffer can hardly avoid referring to the dogmas formulated by the early Church. From the battles of those days to preserve the true faith from all threats, there

[98] *Ibid.*, 52. [99] *Ibid.*, 53.
[100] *Ibid.*, 60-1.
[101] *Ibid.*, 71-6. Our single word 'history' can be rendered in German as either *Geschichte* or *Historie*. Present-day theologians like playing with this distinction, which may be expressed as that between 'history as reality' and 'history as science', in the terms used by Maurice Blondel.

developed what he calls a 'critical or negative Christology', which, for him, must always serve simply as a framework for the 'positive' Christology to be found in the Church's living preaching and her sacraments.[102] He gives an outline of what this should be, in terms of the incarnate Word in his humiliation and his exaltation.[103]

During the semester immediately preceding that in which he gave this course in Christology, he had dealt with the problem of the creation and the fall, and later published this under the title *Schöpfung und Fall*.[104] It is a theological commentary on the first three chapters of Genesis, drawing its inspiration from Luther, and making use of the work of the exegete Kantz. It was not, therefore, directly a study of Christology. I mention it here however, not simply because it should receive some kind of mention in any presentation of Bonhoeffer's work as a whole, but because it was entirely written in the conviction that it is only 'by starting from the end'—that end by which the Church lives, and whose name is Jesus Christ—that we can know the meaning of the beginning described in these first pages of the Bible. For Bonhoeffer, indeed, this is the Bible's own viewpoint; it must be read from beginning to end in a Christological perspective. Not, of course, that we must overlook the approaches of philology and history; but the facts they establish can only find their ultimate meaning in the faith of the Church, which finds in them evidence of the latter-day Revelation that constitutes its own life.

Similarly, having briefly recalled Adam's temptation, it is the triple temptation of Christ, and the temptation he is still undergoing in 'his own', which forms the cornerstone of the small book *Versuchung* (Temptation) that resulted from the discussions during a reunion of former students of Finkenwalde in April 1937.[105]

In another small book, *Das Gebetbuch der Bibel. Eine Einführung in die Psalmen* (Bible Prayerbook; an Introduction to the Psalms), which was the last thing published in Bonhoeffer's lifetime, he explains why and how the psalms are the Church's

[102] *Ibid.*, 77.
[103] *Ibid.*, 110-118.
[104] Munich, 1937.
[105] Munich, 1953, and Geneva, 1961.

favourite prayers.[106] The main reason for this is that Jesus' own prayer builds on all their most important themes. In other words, here is yet another instance of the conviction Bonhoeffer held to the end: the light of Revelation, fully accomplished in Jesus Christ, is the only thing that can show us the whole meaning of Scripture, just as it is the only thing that can explain the meaning of the mystery of the Church and of our own lives.

[106] Salzuflen, 1940.

III

One who Taught Others to Live

THEOLOGY for Bonhoeffer is 'ecclesial knowledge' with no meaning outside a context of faith, and is always a consideration of the Church's action and the decisions it has made—and is still making—in obedience to the divine Word in regard to the various forces that threaten it; the ecclesiological and Christological writings I have cited are directly spiritual in scope. We have become well enough aware that in Bonhoeffer thought and action, reflection and life were always inseparably linked. Furthermore, my first chapter, in which I recalled some of the outstanding traits of his personality and the different commitments in which they were expressed, has given us some acquaintance with him as a master of the spiritual life.

Nonetheless, in addition to his specifically theological studies, his short occasional writings, and his enormous correspondence (of which I have given a few examples), he left several works which can indubitably be classed among the finest examples of spiritual literature. These works date from the period of his ministry in the pastoral seminary of Finkenwalde and the enforced retreat which preceded his imprisonment. They are *Nachfolge* (published in English as *The Cost of Discipleship*) and *Gemeinsames Leben* (*Life Together*), and lastly the *Ethics*, which seems to me to be decidedly a work of spirituality in the widest sense of the word. I want now to look at some of the major themes in these important books.

Following Jesus

The title of the first of these books is not easy to translate. In the French edition the difficulty was avoided by substituting for it the title of the first chapter: *Die teure Gnade*, felicitously translated as *Le Prix de la Grâce*. This solution is all the more legitimate in that the themes of the 'price of grace', of 'grace as dearly bought', and the danger of 'getting grace on the cheap', together really sum up what the book is about. However the title chosen by Bonhoeffer himself for the German edition in 1937 expresses its contents more perfectly.

One might be tempted to translate *Nachfolge* as 'Imitation', especially when it is remembered that *The Imitation of Christ* in German is called *Nachfolge Christi*. Yet our 'imitation' misses the dynamism implied by the German *Nachfolge*; it might even suggest a certain flavour of Pelagianism from which we must preserve Bonhoeffer's ideas at all cost. As we shall also see, he was equally far from any hint of quietism. But it was certainly wise to seek some idea other than that of imitation in which to express the spiritual tradition Bonhoeffer was seeking to define in this book.

For that tradition must be expressed in a movement, the movement that sweeps along whoever has heard Jesus' call to follow him. *Nachfolge* is the movement 'after' Jesus, the effective, active response to the call of Jesus to his disciple: 'Come, follow me.' The English title perhaps expresses it best of all: *The Cost of Discipleship*.

The whole book is directed towards making that call heard once again, and to showing the demands it must inevitably make.

In the preface, Bonhoeffer points out the bankruptcy of any preaching which does not appeal to those to whom it ought to appeal, nor repel those whom it ought to repel, because it is simply going over and over the same well-worn phrases, churning out the same generalized ideas, and never expressing the living presence of Christ. But he does not intend to get bogged down in a morass of criticism, either of himself or of others. We must rather, he thinks, 'try to get away from the poverty and pettiness of our own little convictions and problems, and seek the wealth and splendour which are vouchsafed to us in Jesus Christ'. 'We propose to tell how Jesus calls us to be his disciples'—a call that is at once liberating and supremely demanding. 'If they follow Jesus, men escape from the hard yoke of their own laws, and submit to the kindly yoke of Jesus Christ.' But this is no easy way out, nor does it involve a failure to take Jesus' commandments with the utmost seriousness. The yoke is light only for those who accept it totally and generously. Only they will discover that 'his commandments never seeks to destroy life, but to foster, strengthen and heal it'. Jesus himself alone knows to what exact goal his call will lead us. What we know is that the road he wants us to follow 'will be a road of boundless mercy'. For this reason, 'discipleship means joy'.[1]

The book goes on to try to help us encounter Jesus Christ as revealed to us in the gospels, to make us hear his call, and to draw us to follow him.

The opening theme of 'costly grace', or, literally, 'expensive grace', is not worked out in the fashion of a theoretical consideration; it is a sermon, and a sermon largely concerned with the danger of substituting for the living, demanding Word of God a mere theory which can make it so remote as to be quite reassuring: the danger of putting real life to one side, and comforting ourselves with abstract considerations, of denaturing faith—which is essentially adherence and obedience to a *person*—by turning it into a system of ideas.

> Cheap grace means grace as a doctrine, a principle, a system. . . . Cheap grace therefore amounts to a denial of the living Word of God, in fact a denial of the Incarnation of the Word of God.[2]

Cheap grace is 'the justification of sin without the justification of the sinner' who repents. It provides an illusory dispensation from any genuine conversion which must involve a crucified life in imitation of Christ's.

> Cheap grace is the preaching of forgiveness without requiring repentance, baptism without church discipline, Communion without confession, absolution without personal confession. Cheap grace is grace without discipleship, grace without the cross, grace without Jesus Christ, living and incarnate.[3]

[1] *The Cost of Discipleship*, 30-32.
[2] *Ibid.*, 35. [3] *Ibid.*, 36.

But saving grace, such as Christ offers us, the grace of receiving the message and proclaiming it to men, is costly.

> Costly grace is the treasure hidden in the field; for the sake of it a man will gladly go and sell all that he has. It is the pearl of great price to buy which the merchant will sell all his goods. It is the kingly rule of Christ, for whose sake a man will pluck out the eye which causes him to stumble, it is the call of Jesus Christ at which the disciple leaves his nets and follows him.
>
> Costly grace is the gospel which must be *sought* again and again, the gift which must be *asked* for, the door at which a man must knock.[4]

The fact that it is costly does not prevent its being a grace. Quite the reverse: it manifests its genuineness:

> Such grace is *costly* because it calls us to follow, and it is a *grace* because it calls us to follow *Jesus Christ*. It is costly because it costs a man his life, and it is grace because it gives a man the only true life. It is costly because it condemns sin, and grace because it justifies the sinner. Above all, it is *costly* because it cost God the life of his Son: 'ye were bought at a price', and what has cost God much cannot be cheap for us.[5]

This condemnation of cheap grace and exaltation of costly grace is primarily directed against certain false interpretations of the doctrine of *Sola gratia* upon which the theologies of the Reformation were based, and to which, incidentally, a Catholic can in some senses subscribe. Bonhoeffer never rejects the formula itself; what he deplores is the abuse of it that arises the moment a living message is turned into an abstract doctrine, into a 'system'. His preoccupation, and that of the whole of this book, is to bring home the conviction that the life of faith—with its laws, its certainties, its well-defined demands—is always a movement, our active response to a person addressing us and taking hold of us at every minute of our lives in order to take us ever further. In reply to Professor Skydsgaard's development of the great theme of Augustine: 'Seek to find and find to seek again', Paul VI declared, 'A true Christian can never be motionless.'[6] Bonhoeffer would certainly have assented to that.

[4] *Ibid.*, 36-7. [5] *Ibid.*, 37.
[6] Cf. *Documentation catholique*, LX (1963), 1421-6.

With this in mind, he examines certain lessons from history. Monasticism he sees as having been born out of a renewed awareness of the costliness of grace. But Luther's protests against the monastic life of his day were the result of that same conviction.

> As Christianity spread, and the Church became more secularized, this realization of the costliness of grace gradually faded. The world was Christianized, and grace became its common property. It was to be had at low cost. Yet the Church of Rome did not altogether lose that earlier vision. It is highly significant that the Church was to find room for the monastic movement, and to prevent it from lapsing into schism. Here on the outer fringe of the Church was a place where the older vision was kept alive. Here men still remembered that grace costs, that grace means following Christ. . . . Thus monasticism became a living protest against the secularization of Christianity and the cheapening of grace.[7]

But there was a danger of stopping at that point, of thinking the final solution had been found, of making monasticism a kind of alibi and seeing monks as specialists in Christianity-as-a-demanding-way-of-life whose very existence dispensed other Christians from following the narrow path of the gospel. Correspondingly, for the monks the temptation would be to glory in their spiritual achievements. And so it turned out; such, certainly, was Luther's experience, a man who had himself heard the call of Christ and decided to respond to it by means of the monastic life. His objection came from the fact that what he really found there, in a slightly different guise, was the same world he was trying to escape from. Once again, the encounter with grace 'shattered his whole existence. Once more he must leave his nets and follow.'

> Luther did not hear the word : 'Of course you have sinned, but now everything is forgiven, so you can stay as you are and enjoy the consolations of forgiveness.' No, Luther had to leave the cloister and go back to the world, not because the world in itself was good and holy, but because even the cloister was only a part of the world.[8]

In fact, the struggle he was to have with the world was to be

[7] *The Cost of Discipleship*, 38. [8] *Ibid.*, 40.

far weightier than the original one undertaken by monasticism. For he felt himself called to fight right in its midst, in a 'hand-to-hand conflict'.[9]

However, Protestantism in its turn soon distorted the meaning of his decision, and turned it into a principle of easy salvation. All it retained was the notion that any form of life is naturally holy, that Christian life need be no different from ordinary life, the only distinction being that Christians are lucky enough to be assured from time to time that grace is there to justify anything they may happen to do.

> The world has been made 'Christian', but at the cost of secularizing the Christian religion as never before. The antithesis between the Christian life and the life of bourgeois respectability is at an end. The Christian life comes to mean nothing more than living in the world and as the world, in being no different from the world, in fact, in being prohibited from being different from the world for the sake of grace. The upshot of it all is that my only duty as a Christian is to leave the world for an hour or so on a Sunday morning and go to church to be assured that my sins are all forgiven. . . . It is terrifying to realize what use can be made of a genuine evangelical doctrine. In both cases we have the identical formula—'justification by faith alone'. Yet the misuse of the formula leads to the complete destruction of its very essence.[10]

The disastrous consequences of this distortion are all too evident today. Once again, Bonhoeffer considers the crisis racking the Evangelical Church in Germany.

> Do we also realize that this cheap grace has turned back upon us like a boomerang? The price we are having to pay today in the shape of the collapse of the organized Church is only the inevitable consequence of our policy of making grace available to all at too low a cost. We gave away the Word and sacraments wholesale, we baptized, confirmed and absolved a whole nation unasked and without condition. Our humanitarian sentiment made us give that which was holy to the scornful and unbelieving. We poured forth unending streams of grace. But the call to follow Jesus in the narrow way was hardly ever heard. Where were those truths which impelled the early Church to institute the catechumenate, which

[9] *Ibid.* [10] *Ibid.*, 42.

enabled a strict watch to be kept over the frontier between the Church and the world, and afforded adequate protection for costly grace? . . . What are those three thousand Saxons put to death by Charlemagne compared with the millions of spiritual corpses in our country today? . . . The word of cheap grace has been the ruin of more Christians than any commandment of works.[11]

Bonhoeffer would probably not side with those who give a Lutheran or evangelical dogmatism as their reason for condemning out of hand the overtures of the Taizé community. It would seem that he condemned that kind of dogmatism *a priori* as the very opposite of genuinely Lutheran protest:

So they said [that correct doctrine is all that matters], thinking that we must vindicate our Lutheran heritage by making this grace available on the cheapest and easiest terms. To be 'Lutheran' must mean that we leave the following of Christ to legalists, Calvinists and enthusiasts—and all this for the sake of grace. We justified the world, and condemned as heretics those who tried to follow Christ.[12]

Indeed, this trivializing of grace might be used to clip the wings of those who tried to fly too high:

The only effect that such a word [of easy grace] could have on us was to bar our way to progress, and seduce us to the mediocre level of the world, quenching the joy of discipleship by telling us that we were following a way of our own choosing, that we were spending our strength and disciplining ourselves in vain—all of which was not merely useless, but extremely dangerous. After all, we were told, our salvation had already been accomplished by the grace of God.[13]

In a letter from prison in October 1943, Bonhoeffer comes back to this same idea:

As long as a hundred years ago Kierkegaard said that today Luther would say the opposite of what he said then. I think he was right—with some reservations.[14]

In point of fact, 'there is a wrong way of staying in the world

[11] *Ibid.*, 45-6.
[12] *Ibid.*, 45.
[13] *Ibid.*, 46.
[14] *Letters and Papers from Prison*, 71.

and a wrong way of fleeing from it'.[15] The distortion of ideas which began so well always takes the same course: a doctrine becomes fixed, and thereby all movement is stopped. 'Acquired knowledge cannot be divorced from the existence in which it is acquired' without its meaning being altered.[16] We start applying principles, 'laws', a system, things which fit in with our own mental universe, or that well-planned order that protects our social and individual being—when what we should be doing is letting ourselves hear and respond to a living call that will lead us, by a path of renunciation, to the uncharted land of the promise.

Bonhoeffer describes this constant forward movement, this answer to a call that makes it impossible for the believer ever to fall back upon himself, not only with reference to examples from Christian history, but also to some of the incidents in the gospels: the calling of the apostles, Jesus' dialogues with the rich young man, with the lawyer (who was answered with the parable of the Good Samaritan), and with the three men he met on the way to Jerusalem (Lk 9:57-61). All three show clearly what unconditional dedication to himself Jesus demanded. He forbade those he called, and who were serious in wishing to follow him, any escape into 'interesting' problems, into analyzing 'ethical conflicts', into the luxury of a 'divided mind'. He has not come to solve our problems or to enrich our systems of thought. Instead, what he demands is that we detach ourselves from all our well-worn paths, all our possessions, all our responsibilities (think of the man who asked first to go and bury his father), and let him establish our life on absolutely new foundations. This indeed is the force of his call: it 'at once produces a new situation'. His call has God's own power. 'He could not have done so [called so irresistibly]', explains Bonhoeffer, commenting Luke 9:57-61, 'had he not been the incarnate Son of God. But since he is the Christ, he must make it clear from the start that his word is not an abstract doctrine, but the re-creation of the whole life of man.'[17]

The only response to such an absolute Word can be absolute

[15] *The Cost of Discipleship*, 241.
[16] *Ibid.*, 43. [17] *Ibid.*, 52.

obedience. Obedience is not the product of a faith which could have been present already: it is faith's immediate expression. And such obedience cannot try to drift off into the illusory sphere of some purely interior life. It must be at once 'simple' and direct. It was such simple, straightforward obedience that Jesus demanded from Levi at his counter, or Peter beside his nets, when he told them to leave all things and follow him. But since then we have found ways of mitigating that demand.

> If, as we read our Bibles, we heard Jesus speaking to us in this way today we should probably try to argue ourselves out of it like this: 'It is true that the demand of Jesus is definite enough, but I have to remember that he never expects us to take his commands legalistically. What he really wants me to have is faith. But my faith is not necessarily tied up with riches or poverty or anything of the kind. We may be both poor and rich in the spirit. It is not important that I should have no possessions, but if I do I must keep them as though I had them not, in other words I must cultivate a spirit of inward detachment, so that my heart is not in my possessions.'[18]

It is quite true that basically Jesus demands only that we adhere to him in faith, and that this or that individual act is not important as such. But we cannot for that reason so interpret his practical demands as to make them bear simply upon our intentions and interior attitudes. What Jesus asks of us is never *less* than the literal meaning of his commands, but always something more.

> Anyone who does not feel that he would be much happier were he only permitted to understand the commandments of Jesus in a straightforward literal way, and e.g. surrender all his possessions at his bidding rather than cling to them, has no right to this paradoxical interpretation of Jesus' words. We have to hold the two together in mind all the time.[19]

Thus 'simple', unswerving obedience is the true hermeneutic principle, the only attitude which makes it possible for us to hear the Word of salvation by placing ourselves at the disposal of the authority of him who speaks it, whereas all the 'interpretations'

[18] *Ibid.*, 69. [19] *Ibid.*, 72.

we give ourselves, however magnificent a doctrine of grace we may arrive at, leave us at the mercy of our own threadbare points of view and all the blind alleys of escape they provide us with.[20]

Just as the faith of a disciple does not mean letting himself be soothed by the comforting word of cheap grace, but is expressed in practical obedience, so the mission Jesus entrusts him with is not only, or even primarily, one of preaching, but of witness. Those Jesus calls to follow him must *be* the salt of the earth.

> "Ye *are* the salt', not 'Ye *have* the salt'. By identifying the salt with the apostolic proclamation the Reformers robbed the saying of all its sting. No, the word speaks of their whole existence in so far as it is grounded anew in the call of Christ, that same existence which was the burden of the Beatitudes. The call of Christ makes those who respond to it the salt of the earth in their total existence.[21]

The same must be said of the Christian community created by Christ's call, which thus becomes the 'light of the world'. That light is not simply something the community must hold aloft by its words. We must *be* the light, and if we cannot be seen to be it, then we are betraying our call.

> 'Ye are the light'. . . . Flight into the invisible is a denial of the call. A community of Jesus which seeks to hide itself has ceased to follow him. 'Neither do men light a lamp and put it under a bushel, but on the stand'. . . . The bushel may be the fear of man, or perhaps a deliberate conformity to the world for some ulterior motive, a missionary purpose for example, or a sentimental humanitarianism. But the motive may be more sinister than that; it may be a 'Reformation theology' which boldly claims the name of *theologia crucis*, and pretends to prefer to Pharisaic ostentation a modest invisibility, which in practice means conformity to the world.[22]

These particular ideas of Bonhoeffer's are ones we seldom hear quoted nowadays. Nor must we take them as the only basis for his teaching on the Christian life. In fact we have already seen how impossible it is to reduce that teaching to a few general prin-

[20] *Ibid.*, 73-4. [21] *Ibid.*, 105.
[22] *Ibid.*, 106-7.

ciples; and indeed he himself makes clear how necessary it is to keep criticizing and correcting everything we say, however true it may be in itself. Above all let us adopt his concern to study every aspect of the gospels, without ever watering down any one of them.[23]

The experience of brotherhood

'Through the call of Jesus, men become individuals', unique persons, bearing the responsibility for their own responses.[24] In this sense, they are established by him in solitude. Abraham remains the exemplar of the believer, the man who gives his assent to the divine Word. And he is a 'lonely and solitary figure'.[25]

Yet, 'though we all have to enter upon discipleship alone, we do not remain alone'. Whoever has left home, brothers, sisters, mother, father, children or land for the sake of Jesus and his gospel will receive a hundredfold even now. The experience of brotherhood is a great grace, but is also a sphere in which new demands will be made on the disciple of Jesus Christ.[26]

The Cost of Discipleship gives a very clear account of that grace and those demands. But both are shown even more clearly in the short work *Life Together*.

The community life which Jesus' disciples can have the joy of experiencing is an outstanding grace. Of course the Christian's life, like Christ's own, is normally lived in the midst of the world, in adversity and sometimes in isolation. However, the New Testa-

[23] As for preaching, Bonhoeffer considered that it should reproduce, or rather, continue, Jesus' call, with all its urgency and actuality. It should be aimed at coming to grips with life, to stimulate and thus renew it. It should not be content with working out generalities. It has no meaning unless it is done with authority—like Christ's own word, the word of the Church should produce conversion. 'Nor is it enough simply to deplore in general terms that the sinfulness of man infects even his good works. It is necessary to point out concrete sins, and to punish and condemn them.' For preaching goes hand in hand with the power of the keys which is a power of 'binding' as well as 'loosing'. (*The Cost of Discipleship*, 260; see also 59-60. *G.S.*, I, 145 [*No Rusty Swords*, 162].)

[24] *The Cost of Discipleship*, 84.

[25] *Ibid.*, 88. [26] *Ibid.*, 90-91.

ment shows us how 'the prisoner, the sick person, the Christian in exile sees in the companionship of a fellow-Christian a physical sign of the gracious presence of the triune God'.[27] Those who have the privilege of community life have that support and consolation all the time. Their situation is not typical: 'Between the death of Christ and the Last Day it is only by a gracious anticipation of the last things that Christians are privileged to live in visible fellowship with other Christians.'[28]

But it is important to understand the nature of this kind of experience of brotherhood. The community brought together by Christ's call is radically different from those based on any of the more or less clear kinds of natural call. Bonhoeffer stresses the fact that 'Christian community is a spiritual [pneumatic] and not a psychic reality', taking up the distinction used by St Paul. Its mainspring, in other words, is the Spirit of God, not the spontaneous urges of the human soul. It can survive and even grow stronger despite all the disappointments of the natural man, who only seeks for a direct communion or perhaps rather a kind of fusion, in which the ultimate object is the exaltation of self. Not that Christians are immune from the temptation of seeing the community of brotherhood that faith opens to them in that light, just as they frequently mistake warmth of emotion for spirituality. However, 'just as the Christian should not be constantly feeling his spiritual pulse, so, too, the Christian community has not been given to us by God for us to be constantly taking its temperature'.[29] Real Christian community life can even grow deeper as a result of obstacles and difficulties. For the relationships it crystallizes are, to the extent that they are genuine, 'mediate' ones: that is to say, they always exist through each person's relation to Jesus Christ.

Bonhoeffer stresses this even more in *The Cost of Discipleship*, opening up in this regard perspectives not normally seen upon the 'mediation' of Christ—perspectives it is helpful to recall in relation to his reflexions upon the necessity of being open to the world

[27] *Life Together*, 9. [28] *Ibid.*, 8.
[29] *Ibid.*, 18.

and upon Christian life as living-for-others. On Luke 14:26 ('If anyone comes to me and does not hate his own father . . .'), he writes:

> It is no arbitrary choice on the disciple's part, but Christ himself, who compels him thus to break with his past. . . . By virtue of his incarnation he has come between man and his natural life. There can be no turning back, for Christ bars the way. By calling us he has cut us off from all immediacy with the things of this world. He wants to be the centre, through him alone all things shall come to pass. He stands between us and God, and for that very reason he stands between us and all other men and things.[30]

Bonhoeffer could foresee even then the false interpretations that would later be placed upon what he was saying:

> It is theological error of the first magnitude to exploit the doctrine of Christ the Mediator so as to justify direct relationships with the things of this world. It is sometimes argued that if Christ is the Mediator he has borne all the sin which underlies our direct relationships with the world and that he has justified us in them. Jesus has reconciled us to God; we can then, it is supposed, return to the world and enjoy our direct relation with it with a good conscience—although that world is the very world which crucified Christ. This is to equate the love of God with the love of the world. . . . The saying of Christ about hating our immediate relationships is thus turned into a cheerful affirmation of the 'God-given realities of this world'. Once again the justification of the sinner has become the justification of sin.[31]

The 'mediate' nature of the fraternal relationship is the criterion of the truly 'pneumatic' community founded upon a common call from Christ. It is the mark of genuinely spiritual love.

> [Spiritual love will make a man] respect the line that has been drawn between him and us by Christ, and it will find full fellowship with him in the Christ who alone binds us together. Thus this spiritual love will speak to Christ about a brother more than to a brother about Christ.[32]

Because it is founded only on the call from Christ, the genuine brotherly community can only be understood as a cell of the

[30] *The Cost of Discipleship*, 84-5.
[31] *Ibid.*, 87. [32] *Life Together*, 23.

universal Church. Only in this way can it avoid the temptation to smugness which would reduce it to the level of a merely natural, 'psychic' community. Only in this way can it avoid sectarianism.

> Life together under the Word will remain sound and healthy only where it does not form itself into a movement, an order, a society, a *collegium pietatis*, but rather, where it understands itself as being a part of the one, holy, catholic, Christian Church, where it shares actively and passively in the sufferings and struggles and promise of the whole Church. Every principle of selection and every separation connected with it that is not necessitated quite objectively by common work, local conditions, or family connections is of the greatest danger to a Christian community. When the way of intellectual or spiritual selection is taken, the human element always insinuates itself and robs the fellowship of its spiritual power and effectiveness for the Church, drives it into sectarianism.[33]

To indicate both what are the graces and what the demands of community life for disciples of Christ, Bonhoeffer considers the key moments of the day—not in relation to special feasts, but of the regular daily round.

This follows the rhythm of nature which for Christians holds its own special symbolism.

> The Old Testament day begins at evening and ends with the going down of the sun. It is the time of expectation. The day of the New Testament Church begins with the break of day and ends with the dawning light of the next morning. It is the time of fulfilment, the resurrection of the Lord. At night Christ was born, a light in darkness; noonday turned to night when Christ suffered and died on the Cross. But in the dawn of Easter morning Christ rose in victory from the grave. . . . The early morning belongs to the Church of the risen Christ. At the break of day it remembers the morning on which death and sin lay prostrate in defeat and new life and salvation were given to mankind.[34]

Thus the act of worship with which the community's day opens is made up of elements familiar to all Christian tradition: the singing of psalms, a reading (generally consecutive day by day) from Scripture, church hymns, and prayer of a more flexible

[33] *Ibid.*, 24. [34] *Ibid.*, 27.

kind to express the faith and needs of the community. While stressing the meaning and importance of these various elements, Bonhoeffer even goes so far as to give practical details on how best to read the Bible intelligibly without imposing one's own subjective personality on it, and the technique of hymn-singing which must always be 'the sung *Word*'.

> The fact that we do not speak it but sing it only expresses the fact that our spoken words are inadequate to express what we want to say, that the burden of our song goes far beyond all human words. Yet we do not hum a melody; we sing words of praise to God, words of thanksgiving, confession, and prayer. Thus the music is completely the servant of the Word. It elucidates the Word in its mystery.[35]

That is why liturgical singing is generally in unison. The inspiration of those who introduce a second voice on their own initiative is misplaced, as is also the liberty taken by others of singing an octave higher or lower—whether in order to show off their voices or to avoid making any effort.[36] These comments are a very good example of Bonhoeffer's keen sense of the concrete in every sphere, of expression and of the symbolic value of actions and of words. He was never a man of ideas alone.

As we have seen, brotherly life does not exclude individual life, but presupposes and in fact fosters it. 'Let him who cannot be alone beware of community. . . . But the reverse is also true: Let him who is not community beware of being alone.'[37] Life in any community should always protect the individual, interior life of each of its members. That is why silence is as important an element in it as speech, through which communication takes place.

> The mark of solitude is silence, as speech is the mark of community. Silence and speech have the same inner correspondence and difference as do solitude and community. One does not exist without the other. Right speech comes out of silence, and right silence comes out of speech.[38]

For silence is not an absolute, nor is every kind of speech worth having. 'There is such a thing as forbidden, self-indulgent silence,

[35] *Ibid.*, 43.
[36] *Ibid.*, 43-4.
[37] *Ibid.*, 57-8.
[38] *Ibid.*, 58-9.

a proud, offensive silence.'[39] We all need to examine the quality of our silences. But a well-run community will always have fixed times for quiet.

> Where a family live close together in a constricted space and the individual does not have the quietness he needs, regular times of quiet are absolutely necessary. After a time of quiet we meet others in a different and a fresh way. Many a household fellowship will be able to provide for the individual's needs to be alone, and thus preserve the fellowship itself from injury, only by adopting a regular order.[40]

There is at least one thing which every member of a fraternal community must have which requires silence, and that is individual 'meditation', made up of 'Scriptures, private prayer and intercession'. Here, once again, Bonhoeffer does not hesitate to go into details and give practical advice: one must be faithful to the time fixed despite aridity of soul, one must even make use of distractions as subject-matter for dialogue with God, there must be no self interest, no making one's prayer, for instance, merely a preparation for the next sermon, but only attentiveness to God's Word spoken individually to oneself. . . . Prayer does not, of course, have any hard and fast rules, but there are certain conditions and practical requirements which we must be aware of, and to which we must have the humility to submit. Abstraction from reality is as much out of place in our inner search for God as in our service of him in the world.[41]

A consideration of how demanding and how noble is the service of God through the service of others forms another chapter of the small book, *Life Together*. The spirit of service must rectify, and sometimes actually reverse our spontaneous natural urge to rival other people in aggressiveness or struggle for position. Jesus recognized and expected such rivalries among his disciples (cf. Lk 9:46 ff.). The first corrective will be provided by controlling one's tongue, as recommended in the Epistle of James. But at a deeper level, every Christian's attitude must be determined by faith in

[39] *Ibid.*, 60. [40] *Ibid.*
[41] *Ibid.*, 61-8.

God our Creator who has made us all with our differences, and God our Redeemer who has saved us all by his grace. This conviction should enable us to retain at once our humility, our spirit of service and our sense of gratitude. And in this regard Bonhoeffer quotes fom *The Imitation of Christ*: 'Never think that thou hast made any progress till thou look upon thyself as inferior to all.' Once one is convinced of this, then one is ready to listen to others, for 'listening can be a greater service than speaking'. One will also be at the disposal of others, ungrudging of one's time in their service, and not always convinced that one's own affairs are of greater importance than theirs.[42]

Above all, the fraternal community presupposes mutual support, inspired by the same patience that God shows to us. It is not the support of mere passivity. For, though a brother must know when to be silent in regard to another's failings, he must also know when to speak out. He must respect the other's privacy, while yet avoiding the murderous opting out of Cain: 'Am I my brother's keeper?' Fraternal correction has its regular place in community life, and finds its true meaning when each member sees himself as he is before God, realizing that he needs both advice and comfort.

> Nothing can be more compassionate than the severe rebuke that calls a brother back from the path of sin. It is a ministry of mercy, an ultimate offer of genuine fellowship, when we allow nothing but God's word to stand between us, judging and succouring.[43]

It is this same ideal of service which gives meaning to authority within the community. Here again 'immediacy' is suspect. Speaking of bishops, the New Testament does not speak in praise of

> worldly charm and the brilliant attributes of a spiritual personality. The bishop is a simple, faithful man, sound in faith and life, who rightly discharges his duty to the Church. . . . The Church does not need brilliant personalities, but faithful servants of Jesus and the brethren.[44]

More profound than fraternal correction is confession, which

[42] *Ibid.*, 69-77.
[43] *Ibid.*, 83.
[44] *Ibid.*, 85.

effects that constant regeneration needed in any community of sinful men. Through it there is brought about a return to membership in the community, the passover of the cross, and entry to new life. 'What happened to us in baptism is bestowed upon us anew in confession.' We receive the certainty of forgiveness. But for that certainty there must first be an admission of '*concrete* sins'.[45]

It is vital, however, that confession be seen in the light of faith. Just as the confessor is quite different from the psychologist, and the sinner a man who lives wholly by divine mercy, so too the act of confessing is not simply a 'good work' which produces its effect automatically, but the acceptance of God's promises, 'God's offer of grace, help and forgiveness'.

That is why the ultimate purpose of confession is to prepare 'for the common reception of holy Communion'.

> The day of the Lord's supper is an occasion of joy for the Christian community. Reconciled in their hearts with God and the brethren, the congregation receives the gift of the body and blood of Jesus Christ, and, receiving that, it receives forgiveness, new life and salvation. It is given new fellowship with God and men. The fellowship of the Lord's supper is the superlative fulfilment of Christian fellowship. As the members of the congregation are united in body and blood at the table of the Lord so will they be together in eternity. Here the community has reached its goal. Here joy in Christ and his community is complete. The life of Christians together under the Word has reached its perfection in the sacrament.[46]

Beyond good or evil

Though they contain teaching of universal application, the instructions Bonhoeffer gave in the pastoral seminary at Finkenwalde (published in *The Cost of Discipleship* and *Life Together*) were primarily directed to a very specialized audience living in fairly unusual conditions. Bonhoeffer gave himself totally to these men who had been placed in his care. Yet he never thought it possible to limit his horizons to this circle of 'brothers', this single

[45] *Ibid.*, 90-91. [46] *Ibid.*, 94-6.

community, however alive and real it was. The moment the government removed him from his work as director and moving spirit at Finkenwalde, he set about writing the book that was, as I have said, closest of all to his heart—the *Ethics*—which was to provide the foundations for, and outline the features of, a genuinely human and Christian way of life in a far wider context than the two preceding works.

Just as Emmanuel Mounier spent his time in prison writing his masterly *Traité du caractère*, so Bonhoeffer spent his years of confinement from 1939 to 1943 in setting down his considerations about man, whose human 'face' he also saw as being gravely in danger, about man's true status in the world and society, about his heritage and his vocation. In the period of anguish and upheaval which each lived through, Mounier and Bonhoeffer both felt their most urgent task to be one of fundamental education.

Both works remain unfinished—not in the sense of early, completed chapters waiting for later ones to follow, but in the sense of more or less fully developed reflexions that were to be fitted into a gradually maturing whole and might never perhaps be regarded as final. Whether or no, both works, though quite dissimilar, have come down to us in a form that is still well suited to stimulate our thinking and stir us out of any possible lethargy.

Bonhoeffer's *Ethics*, a complex and sometimes extremely difficult work, is not a purely theoretical study of man in himself, nor of the objective laws governing good and evil. This is clear at once from the title he planned for the first section: 'Ethics as formation'; his reflexions in fact begin precisely from the statement that any 'theoretical and systematic' ethic must be inadequate. This does not, however, mean that we can be satisfied simply with following whatever rules enable us to live as comfortably as possible. Ours is an age concerned above all with concrete reality.[47]

[47] A concrete ethic, striving to remain faithful to the reality of things and of situations, does not necessarily mean giving way to relativism. Bonhoeffer illustrates this in relation to lying and telling the truth. Truth is always spoken to someone. What is the use of a truth which, failing to take proper account of the hearer, actually misleads him? A lie is a betrayal of reality. And Bonhoeffer thinks that there are exceptional cases of truths which can only be said and heard in confession. (*Ethics*, 363 ff.).

But such reality can also be seen to have depths so great as to show up the inadequacy of the carefully cut-and-dried categories of classical ethics, even apart from the possible ambiguities that may arise in any given situation to which we apply them. Ours is a world that produces not simply men who are more or less moral or immoral, but 'villains and saints' who 'tear open the infernal or the divine abyss'.

> It is worse for a liar to tell the truth than for a lover of truth to tell a lie. . . . The most shining virtues of him who has fallen away are as black as night in comparison with the darkest lapses of the steadfast.[48]

In this apocalyptic universe, which Bonhoeffer goes on to examine, all the attitudes history presents us with can do no more than serve to guide our action. All are doomed to fail: the attitude of the 'reasonable' man, of the 'fanatic', of the man with a 'conscience', of the 'man of duty', of the man who believes in 'absolute freedom' or in 'private virtuousness'—all of them seem to him to merge together into the tragi-comic position of a Quixote:

> That is how it looks when an old world ventures to take up arms against a new one and when a world of the past hazards an attack against the superior forces of the commonplace and mean.[49]

The only attitude that brings peace is that which combines simplicity with discernment: that paradoxical behaviour which Jesus himself recommended, uniting the 'wisdom of the serpent' with the 'innocence of the dove' (Mt 10:16). But this presupposes the ability 'to look in freedom at God and at reality'.[50]

In effect the only ideal can be a contradiction, unless the attitude adopted is based on the recognition of him who reconciles God and the reality of the world, him whose work effects a total renewal in our way of approaching all the problems of life. 'The point of departure for Christian ethics', the only possible way of making sense of a life whose whole meaning has been brought into question in our day, 'is not the reality of one's own self, or the reality of the world; nor is it the reality of standards and values.

[48] *Ethics*, 64-5. [49] *Ibid.*, 67-8.
[50] *Ibid.*, 69.

It is the reality of God as He reveals Himself in Jesus Christ.'[51]

From this standpoint, it may be said that Christian ethics lies beyond good and evil. It places these constitutive concepts of morality in the context of a vision of things which alters their meaning so radically that one may even wonder to what extent the notion of Christian ethics is meaningful at all.

> The knowledge of good and evil seems to be the aim of all ethical reflection. The first task of Christian ethics is to invalidate this knowledge. In launching this attack on the underlying assumptions of all other ethics, Christian ethics stands so completely alone that it becomes questionable whether there is any purpose in speaking of Christian ethics at all.[52]

The Bible indeed connects the knowledge of good and evil with estrangement from God, and man's desire to make himself God's equal (cf Gen 3 : 5)

This does not, of course, mean that Christian ethics demands a return to the spontaneity of natural instinct. There are times, indeed, when Bonhoeffer lays great stress on the purifying role played by 'reason', and of the Age of Enlightenment which so valued it, in our perception of the ethical demands made upon us. But he always makes a point at the same time of showing the formal, abstract nature of its processes, for 'intellectual clarity is often achieved at the expense of insight into reality'.[53] Indeed, as Bergson had noted earlier, if it is true that 'reason intervenes in a regulating capacity in a reasoning being', then to try to make it the principle of the whole movement of life, and above all of the moral obligation that actually governs life, amounts to 'believing that it is the fly-wheel that make the machine run'.[54] Thus Bonhoeffer is convinced that a truly human decision is always above and beyond any 'reasons' we may be able to give for it, for it is only within that decision, so to say, that the reasons have

[51] *Ibid.*, 189-90. [52] *Ibid.*, 17.
[53] *Ibid.*, 97; cf. 273-4.
[54] H. Bergson, *Les Deux Sources de la morale et de la religion*, Paris, 1932, p. 17.

force. In realizing this, one is also avoiding the error of seeing intelligence as something exterior to the decision to act.

> The decision between the clearly-known good and the clearly-known evil excludes human knowledge itself from the decision; it transposes the ethical into the struggle between the knowledge, which is already oriented towards the good, and the will which still offers resistance, and it thereby fails to bring about that authentic decision in which the whole man, complete with his knowledge and his will, seeks and finds the good in the equivocal complexity of a historical situation solely through the venture of the deed.[55]

The Christian ethic does not relate to the infra-intellectual areas of animal or purely social life, but to the supra-rational order of faith. 'Faith in this Jesus Christ is the sole fountain-head of all good.'[56] The Christian can say that 'Jesus Christ has become my conscience'.[57]

Far from recommending any blindfold decisions, it requires the 'preparing of the way', as is clearly shown from several passages in Scripture (Is 40:4; Mic 2:13; Ps 107:16; Lk 3:4 ff). 'The way must be made ready for the Word. It is the Word itself that demands it.' There is preparation for the ways of grace, even though that preparation may be something more than a merely human 'programme', even though what we are preparing is not our way to Christ, but Christ's way to us.[58]

The most important thing to note is that the supra-intellectual order of faith is primarily something concrete, the order of reality. The divine Word which calls forth faith, as Bonhoeffer tells us in his earlier book, *The Cost of Discipleship*, is 'a re-creation of the whole life of man'.[59] So Christian ethics, which in a sense is the definition of life as remoulded by faith, concerns the whole life of man:

> We live by responding to the word of God which is addressed to us in Jesus Christ. Since this word is addressed to our entire life,

[55] *Ethics*, 215. [56] *Ibid.*, 213.
[57] *Ibid.*, 244. [58] *Ibid.*, 134 ff.
[59] Cf. *supra*, 78.

the response, too, can only be an entire one; it must be given with our entire life. . . . The life which confronts us in Jesus Christ as a 'yes' and a 'no' to our life, requires the response of a life which assimilates and unites this 'yes' and this 'no'.[60]

Among Bonhoeffer's major preoccupations was the struggle against all forms of dualism, whether in life or in thought. He dedicates a whole sub-section of the *Ethics* to attacking what he calls 'thinking in terms of two spheres', a mistake which seems to him to have for far too long tainted Christian ethics, based on the 'conception of a juxtaposition and conflict of two spheres, the one divine, holy, supernatural and Christian, and the other worldly, profane, natural and un-Christian'.

Reality as a whole now falls into two parts, and the concern of ethics is with the proper relation of these two parts to each other. In the scholastic scheme of things the realm of the natural is made subordinate to the realm of grace; in the pseudo-Lutheran scheme the autonomy of the orders of this world is proclaimed in opposition to the law of Christ, and in the scheme of the Enthusiasts the congregation of the elect takes up the struggle with a hostile world for the establishment of God's kingdom on earth. In all these schemes the cause of Christ becomes a partial and provincial matter within the limits of reality.[61]

This Bonhoeffer wants at all costs to avoid. It is not that he envisages a merging of the reality of God and all that belongs to him with the realities of the world. The reality penetrated by God requires our 'no' as well as our 'yes'. As we have already seen, in quoting from this same section of the *Ethics*, the Church needs her own 'definite space'.[62] The witness we must give to Jesus Christ, Lord of the world 'can be delivered in the right way only if it springs from a hallowed life in the congregation of God'.[63] We must not forget that 'there is a love for the world which is enmity towards God (Jas 4:4)'.[64] What Bonhoeffer is attacking is the system of 'static antagonism' between God and the world,

[60] *Ethics*, 222.
[61] *Ibid.*, 196.
[62] Cf. *supra*, 65.
[63] *Ethics*, 203; cf. 298-300.
[64] *Ibid.*, 204.

which fails to take account of the fact that 'in Christ the reality of God entered into the reality of the world'.[65] This in fact is the mystery of the Body of Christ.[66]

The higher unity achieved in a way of life founded upon faith and transcending the simple opposition between good and evil, rests upon the work of reconciliation with God accomplished in Christ Jesus. It is Christ who brings to an end the state of divided conscience in which men have lived from the first, a state in which they cannot possibly attain to their true end, nor even resolve their problems to discover reality. Only he who is capable of recognizing that there is 'only one reality, and that is the reality of God, which has become manifest in Christ in the reality of the world',[67] only such a man is enabled to confront the tasks of life with resolution. Only the man of faith can avoid being that 'man of two souls' spoken of in James 1:8. He alone escapes those 'conflicts of ethical decision' which are in themselves insoluble, for the motives which drive conscience to determine upon action find their determining value only in relation to a life-purpose, a total perspective, which is larger than they are.[68] Only the believer is above and beyond the dilemma of a Kantian moral 'formalism' which ignores the intrinsic worth of 'things' (for as Péguy put it, Kant 'had no hands'), and an 'expediency' which can provide no criterion for 'success'.[69] He alone escapes the twofold trap of a 'radicalism' which rides roughshod over concrete realities as they appear in all the complexity of historical fact, and the spirit of 'compromise' so often resorted to in casuistry which sets aside demands of the Word of God, from which there can be no dispensation, as well as the 'simplicity' of living according to the gospel.[70]

But, surely, the elements of a Christian ethic conceived in this fashion are too impermanent? One can hardly think the ethic Bonhoeffer is proposing a realistic one? The answer to this problem will clearly depend upon our understanding—and certainly

[65] *Ibid.*, 60; cf. 198, 201.
[66] *Ibid.*, 205.
[67] *Ibid.*, 197.
[68] *Ibid.*, 68.
[69] *Ibid.*, 85, 193-5, 226, 282-3.
[70] *Ibid.*, 127-30.

also our experience—of reality. Bonhoeffer himself is constantly reiterating what reality means to him. The reality he bases all his thinking upon is reality manifested and given back to itself through the Revelation and reconciliation effected in Jesus Christ. Furthermore, his fundamental ideas, though they may sometimes seem abstract or other-worldly, are interspersed and illustrated by references to words, deeds and attitudes of Jesus, or other lessons from the New Testament, which make them surprisingly authoritative. And, conversely, these scriptural texts acquire in this new context a significance and scope which are not always quite so easy to recognize. I have mentioned what Bonhoeffer says about the wisdom of serpents and the simplicity of doves—which is in fact one of the *leitmotivs* of the book—and also the passage from Genesis on the knowledge of good and evil. Here, as in *The Cost of Discipleship*, Bonhoeffer shows how Jesus did not let himself be impaled upon the dilemmas of conscience which the Pharisees and Saducees used to try to entrap him; he also refers us to Chapter 11 of Matthew, to the story of the Good Samaritan (Lk 10 : 25), to the disputes about the observance of the Sabbath (Mt 12 : 11), and other texts of similar importance.

> What takes place between Jesus and the Pharisees is only a repetition of that first temptation of Jesus (Mt 4 :1-11), in which the devil tries to lure him into a disunion in the word of God, and which Jesus overcomes by virtue of his essential unity with the word of God. And this temptation of Jesus in its turn has its prelude in the question with which the serpent in Paradise ensnares Adam and Eve and brings about their downfall : 'Yea, hath God said?' It is the question which implies all the disunion against which man is powerless, because it constitutes his essential character, the question which can be overcome (but not answered) only from beyond this disunion. . . . In the New Testament there is no single question which Jesus answers with an acceptance of the human either-or that every such question implies.[71]

For Jesus did not in fact come to solve men's problems, but to save them.[72] Generally speaking, he never let himself be caught in

[71] *Ibid.*, 29. [72] *Ibid.*, 355.

the kind of alternatives with which human life is so often faced: 'Man, who made me a judge or divider over you?' (Lk 12:14), he replied brusquely when asked to be the arbiter in a dispute. 'Judge not, that ye be not judged' (Mt 7:1) he commanded his disciples, on another occasion. And it is evidently a very different type of judgment that Paul is referring to when he declares: 'The spiritual man judges all things, but is himself to be judged by no one' (I Cor 2:14): here it is that supremely simple act of the man who is no longer divided in soul, who knows but one thing, 'Jesus Christ, and him crucified' (I Cor 2:2).[73]

The Christian ethic Bonhoeffer outlines can be summed up in a single idea; conformity, or better perhaps conformation, to Jesus Christ. It is an ethic that grows out of contemplation: *Ecce homo.*[74] Its problem is the very precise one of knowing 'the way in which Christ takes form among us here and now'.[75] And Christ is, equally precisely, at once 'the Incarnate, Crucified and Risen'.[76] He must be continually formed in our world and our history. But there is also a specific place where this happens: the Church.

> What befell Christ had befallen mankind. It is a mystery for which there is no explanation, that only a part of mankind recognize the form of their Redeemer. The longing of the Incarnate to take form in all men is as yet still unsatisfied. He bore the form of man as a whole, and yet he can take form only in a small band. These are his Church.
>
> 'Formation' consequently means in the first place Jesus's taking form in his Church. . . . The New Testament states the case profoundly and clearly when it calls the Church the Body of Christ. . . . The Church is nothing but a section of humanity in which Christ has really taken form.[77]

If this is so, then the Christian ethic will always and of necessity have the dimensions of the Church:

> The point of departure for Christian ethics is the Body of Christ, the form of Christ in the form of the Church, and the formation of

[73] *Ibid.,* 28-30, 33-4.
[74] *Ibid.,* 70.
[75] *Ibid.,* 85.
[76] *Ibid.,* 81.
[77] *Ibid.,* 83.

the Church in conformity with the form of Christ. . . . Ethics as formation is possible only upon the foundation of the form of Jesus Christ which is present in his Church. The Church is the place where Jesus Christ's taking form is proclaimed and accomplished. It is this proclamation and this event that Christian ethics is designed to serve.[78]

It is still the same basically theological concept of ethics that Bonhoeffer puts forward when, in another passage, he fixes it within the relationship between Christ and the Holy Spirit:

> The problem of Christian ethics is the realization among God's creatures of the revelational reality of God in Christ. . . . The place which in all other ethics is occupied by the antithesis of 'should be' and 'is', idea and accomplishment, motive and performance, is occupied in Christian ethics by the relation of reality and realization, past and present, history and event (faith), or, to replace the equivocal concept by the unambiguous name, the relation of Jesus Christ and the Holy Spirit.[79]

The will of God

There is another relationship, however, which helps both to illumine the meaning of Christian ethics and to make its content clearer: that between Christ and the will of the Father. As I have said, we never find any hesitancy in Jesus's behaviour, any doubt among different possible courses, any pause, any scruple, but always a firm and assured step which sets his decision from the first above any conflict of conscience. This is because he has a point of reference which is stability itself—the will of him who has sent him.

> The freedom of Jesus is not the arbitrary choice of one amongst innumerable possibilities; it consists on the contrary precisely in the complete simplicity of his action, which is never confronted by a plurality of possibilities, conflicts or alternatives, but always only by one thing. This one thing Jesus calls the will of God. He says that to do this will is his meat. This will of God is his life. He lives and acts not by the knowledge of good and evil but by the will of God. There is only one will of God. In it the origin is

[78] *Ibid.*, 84, 88. [79] *Ibid.*, 190.

recovered; in it there is established the freedom and the simplicity of all action.[80]

The only possible object of a Christian ethic, therefore, is the 'commandment' of God in which his will is expressed. But it is important to understand the nature of that commandment. It is, in fact, radically different from any abstract law that defines general principles of action upon which conscience can set to work. It does not involve us either in introspection or in conflicts of conscience.[81] Like God himself, 'it embraces the whole of life. It is not only unconditional; it is also total. It does not only forbid and command; it also permits. It does not only bind; it also sets free; and it does this by binding.'[82]

This total character of God's commandment comes from the fact that it embraces the whole of reality :

> God's commandment is the speech of God to man. Both in its content and in its form it is concrete speech to the concrete man. God's commandment leaves man no room for application or interpretation. It leaves room only for obedience or disobedience. God's commandment cannot be found and known in detachment from time and place; it can only be heard in a local and temporal context. If God's commandment is not clear, definite and concrete to the last detail, then it is not God's commandment.[83]

Embracing all of reality, it is expressed through the basic structures in which that reality has been created and redeemed by God. Those basic structures are what Bonhoeffer calls the 'mandates'; for him the term 'mandate' indicates the task, and the authority that goes with it, that God entrusts to certain institutions in the world in order to co-operate in the work of creation and salvation achieved in Christ. He distinguishes four such 'mandates', the first three belonging to the order of creation and the fourth to that of redemption : the family, work, the State and the Church.[84]

In regard to the first three, we may note how important a place Bonhoeffer gives in his ethical system to the study and

[80] *Ibid.*, 30.
[81] *Ibid.*, 281-2.
[82] *Ibid.*, 277.
[83] *Ibid.*, 278.
[84] *Ibid.*, 207 ff., 286 ff.

appreciation of the 'natural' order. It is true that he refers directly to scripture to determine what the four mandates are; and indeed, the whole natural order only finds its ultimate meaning, and only exists at all, because of its relationship to Christ (cf. John 1:10; Col 1:16). It remains, nonetheless, that he does not think it possible to give a total account of reality, or of human destiny within that reality, if one considers it only in the light of the sin-grace relationship. In this respect he deplores the fact that 'the concept of the natural has fallen into discredit in Protestant ethics'. This of necessity makes it impossible for them to throw any light on the problems of natural life however vital they may be.[85] Though, on the one hand, it must be admitted that there are certain basic elements of human life which in themselves offer no scope for 'moralizing'—there is no occasion for any torment of conscience to discover the need to eat, drink, or sleep[86]—there is, on the other, an order of values which, though relative, are by no means negligible, and which are not directly determined by one's decision to accept or reject the Word of God. This is clear from the distinction we make between the 'natural', i.e. whatever is ordered towards the preservation of life (tainted by sin though it be), and the 'unnatural', i.e. whatever undermines life. Reason, which is part of this natural order, and which also shares in its frailty and the damage done to it by sin, is fitted for grasping its laws. To deny it any value is, ultimately, to destroy the foundations upon which revelation and salvation are communicated to us. For 'Christ himself entered the natural life'.[87]

With this in mind, Bonhoeffer sets out a series of reflexions about 'the natural life', the right of the individual in general, and more especially 'the right to bodily life', 'suicide', 'reproduction and nascent life', 'the freedom of bodily life' and 'the natural rights of the life of the mind'. These sub-sections, though they remain unfinished, are rather similar to those found in the classical

[85] *Ibid.*, 143 ff. [86] *Ibid.*, 268.

[87] *Ibid.*, 145. Similarly, disowning all narrow personalism, he writes: 'The isolation of the person from the world of things is idealistic and not Christian' (*Ethics*, 326; see also 49-50).

treatises of moral theology. They make it clear that, at least for Bonhoeffer, grace does not destroy nature. Furthermore, the behaviour whose principles are worked out in Christian ethics, while always marked by 'simplicity', must, if it is to be authentic, be 'in correspondence with reality'.[88] It is this last that is assured by the three 'mandates' of the family, work, and government, all of which are directed to preserving the order of creation, as is clear from Scripture itself.

The 'mandate' of the Church relates to a different end: the fulfilment of God's saving plan as effected in Jesus Christ. It is carried out not so much alongside the other three as within them —in the sense that the four 'mandates' concern the same actual man, and that the 'mandate' of the Church is (though it is also more than this) to recall to us the duty of fulfilling faithfully and freely the other 'mandates'.[89]

The commandment of God expressed in the four 'mandates', is expressed in the mandate of the Church in two ways: publicly and privately, in preaching which is addressed to everyone, and within the framework of personal confession of sin. These two ways in which God's commandment is manifested are both required for completeness; on the one hand, the liberty of faith must not be jeopardized by the workings of legalistic casuistry, or by imperceptibly drifting into psychology; on the other, the commandment of God must not, in the stating of general ethical principles, lose its power to make practical demands upon us. Bonhoeffer considers Catholicism to be especially threatened by the first of these dangers and Protestantism more likely to succumb to the second.[90]

Above all, the stress on 'simplicity' which is at the basis of all Christian ethics, and which enables the believer to see beyond all conflicts of conscience though submission to the will of God, must not leave us with the idea that this divine will is something we do not have to be continually seeking. To discover it, indeed, should

[88] *Ethics*, 227 ff., 235 ff. [89] *Ibid.*, 211.
[90] *Ibid.*, 292 ff.

be the Christian's constant preoccupation, as Scripture continually reminds us (cf. Rom 2:18; 12:2; Phil 1:9, 10; Eph 5:9 ff.).

> The will of God may lie very deeply concealed beneath a great number of available possibilities. The will of God is not a system of rules which is established from the outset; it is something new and different in each different situation in life, and for this reason a man must ever anew examine what the will of God may be. The heart, the understanding, observation and experience must all collaborate in this task. It is no longer a matter of a man's own knowledge of good and evil, but solely of the living will of God; our knowledge of God's will is not something over which we ourselves dispose, but it depends solely upon the grace of God, and this grace is and requires to be new every morning. That is why this proving or examining of the will of God is so serious a matter.[91]

As has just been said, it mobilizes all our resources, and Bonhoeffer has more to say yet; but above all it presupposes at bottom that 'metamorphosis', that 'renewing of mind' called for in Romans (in the passage quoted earlier, 12:2; see also Eph 5:9), which makes the believer a 'child of God who lives in unity with the will of the Father, in the conformation of the one true Son of God'.[92] And that is also why, in addition to all the human resources which are converted and called to co-operate in discerning the will of God, 'all will be embraced and pervaded by prayer'.[93]

The way to freedom

The Christian ethic, as it has been defined in the preceding pages, is by all accounts an ethic of responsibility—in other words of a liberty that knows itself linked with the will of another being, a will in light of which it makes its decisions, and to whose judgment it submits. Living 'before God' is one of the themes that were to run through Bonhoeffer's thinking right up to the

[91] *Ibid.*, 38. [92] *Ibid.*, 38-9.
[93] *Ibid.*, 40.

end.[94] It really sums up what he means by faith, and in it he also finds strength and consolation.

> The man who acts ideologically sees himself justified in his idea; the responsible man commits his action into the hands of God and lives by God's grace and favour.[95]

In his first draft of a poem called 'Stations on the way to freedom', Bonhoeffer, while himself in prison, describes in condensed form the elements of a life wholly faithful to the human condition, and inspired by faith in God.[96] Eberhard Bethge, for whose birthday the poem was planned, had the happy inspiration of publishing it at the beginning of the *Ethics*. Certainly none of his writings is so well able to give us the quintessence of that quality of Bonhoeffer's that enabled him to teach others so much about how to live.

The first of the four 'stations' is *Discipline* :

> If you set out to seek freedom, then learn above all things
> to govern your soul and your senses, for fear that your passions
> and longings may lead you away from the path you should follow.
> Chaste be your mind and your body, and both in subjection,
> obediently steadfastly seeking the aim set before them;
> only through discipline may a man learn to be free.

The second 'station' is *Action*—action in the concrete sense of actual activity :

> Daring to do what is right, not what fancy may tell you,
> valiantly grasping occasions, not cravenly doubting—
> freedom comes only through deeds, not through thoughts taking wing.
> Faint not nor fear, but go out to the storm and the action,
> trusting in God whose commandment you faithfully follow;
> freedom, exultant, will welcome your spirit with joy.

The third 'station' takes us right to the heart of the mystery of a life set free and illuminated by faith. It is *Suffering*. The value

[94] *Ibid.*, 122 ff., 126 ff., 234, 248 ff., 255; *Letters and Papers from Prison*, 213-14.
[95] *Ethics*, 234.
[96] *Letters and Papers from Prison*, 202-3.

Bonhoeffer sets upon it makes it quite impossible to interpret his ideas about it in any naturalist sense. In the *Ethics* he condemns the superficiality and bleak emptiness of that naturalism which sees death or health as the only meaningful alternatives, for which only the present moment matters, and which can only end in nihilism. 'Slow pain is more feared than death. There is no recognition, there is even contempt, for the value of suffering in giving form to life through the threat of death.'[97] And, in a letter from prison, written a few days after the poem we are considering now, he also says: 'Whether the human deed is a matter of faith or not depends on whether we understand our suffering as an extension of our action and a completion of freedom.'[98]

> A change has come indeed. Your hands, so strong and active,
> are bound; in helplessness now you see your action
> is ended; you sigh in relief, your cause committing
> to stronger hands; so now you may rest contented.
> Only for one blissful moment could you draw near to touch
>   freedom;
> then, that it might be perfected in glory, you gave it to God.

The last 'station' follows directly from this. It is *Death.* Not that Bonhoeffer puts death on a pedestal—rather he deplores the idolatry of death as the precise opposite of faith, as well as being also the denial of all genuine humanism. To idolize death provides a foundation upon which to develop an idolatry of life. Both express the despair of the man enclosed in a proud self-sufficiency, imprisoned within the unbearable limitations of his finitude: only belief in the resurrection makes it possible to see the face of death as it really is, at once merciful and glorious. Faith is not vision, but it does widen our horizons. For those who have faith, ever since the resurrection, though 'it is true that mankind is still living the old life, . . . it is already beyond the old. It still lives in a world of death, but it is already beyond death. It still lives in a world of sin, but it is already beyond sin. The night is not yet

[97] *Ethics*, 107.
[98] *Letters and Papers from Prison*, 206.

over, but already the dawn is breaking.'[99] It is this light that is shining at the end of the way to freedom:

> Come now, thou greatest of feasts on the journey to freedom eternal;
> death, cast aside all burdensome chains, and demolish
> the walls of our temporal body, the walls of our souls that are blinded,
> so that at last we may see that which here remains hidden.
> Freedom, how long we have sought thee in discipline, action, and suffering;
> dying, we now may behold thee revealed in the Lord.

[99] *Ethics*, 79.

IV

A Man of Disturbing Vision

BONHOEFFER is known by his letters from prison, more than by any of the other books we have discussed up to now. They are addressed to his parents, and to his friend Bethge; and we are in a position to understand them far better if we know something of the man (as their recipients did), and if we have traced the way his thought developed during his intense and amazingly varied life. This is especially so in that, in his loneliness in the prison, he often looks back upon his past, upon the heritage he is conscious of bearing, and upon the experiences of his life—thus indicating both the continuity of his preoccupations and the originality of some of his ideas.

Nevertheless it must be recognized that the letters from prison have, simply on their own account, a human interest and a power of suggestion quite adequate to justify the attention they have received. They certainly deserve to be looked at closely for their own sake, though we will naturally read them in the light of everything else we know about the writer.

In describing Bonhoeffer in this final stage of his life as a 'man of disturbing vision', I want to suggest that some of the trains of thought he sketches here could easily lead to disastrous consequences. Some rash people have made him their authority for putting forward an attack on traditional Christianity which practically amounts to destroying it altogether. He himself, as we shall see, was aware of the dangers inherent in any study of obviously incomplete and one-sided reflexions of this kind, developed solely from a critical point of view.[1] But I use the term 'disturbing' in a positive sense as well. These penetrating insights,

[1] Cf. *Letters and Papers from Prison*, 215.

rising out of an extraordinary inner experience and inspired wholly by devotion to the Church's mission and an unconditional fidelity to Jesus Christ, can hardly leave us cold. Though we have every right—indeed a positive duty—to react with certain criticisms, to fill in certain gaps, it can do nothing but good to let ourselves be disturbed by them.

Apocalyptic experience

For this, however, it is vital to understand them rightly. First of all, we must see them in context: not simply in the totality of the life and the witness of their author, but also in the unusual circumstances out of which they grew.

I do not want to discuss only what they may owe to the situation of a man cut off from all normal contact with the outside world, and the narrowing such a situation generally involves. Bonhoeffer himself was the first to recognize, and to suffer from, this absence of dialogue. He constantly begs his correspondents to say honestly what they think, since face-to-face meetings, for which there can really be no substitute, must wait.

But we must remember, too, the apocalyptic atmosphere prevailing in those last months of the war in a Berlin shattered by bombardment. Bonhoeffer describes it in a letter of 30 April 1944:

> I think God is about to accomplish something that, even if we take part in it either outwardly or inwardly, we can only receive with the greatest wonder and awe. Somehow it will be clear—for those who have eyes to see—that Ps. 59:11 b. and Ps. 9:19 f. are true; and we shall have to repeat Jer. 45:5 to ourselves every day.[2]

But it is equally important to bear in mind the way in which Bonhoeffer himself lived out this apocalyptic period. His last thoughts, so often quoted, at which we shall now look closely, grew out of specially prepared ground which must be examined at the same time.

That ground consisted in an intense spiritual life united with

[2] *Ibid.*, 151.

an intellectual life of enormous energy, which neither hard physical conditions nor agonizing uncertainty ever really managed to diminish.

Prayer was the first and last act of his day. The psalms and hymns of Paul Gerhard, the great seventeenth-century hymn-writer, gave him his favourite themes. He was aware of the flavour of pietism they suggested—as did *The Imitation of Christ*, which he also read from time to time in the original Latin. But there is a dimension of individual relationship with Christ which must never be forgotten. Thus he writes of the hymn *Fröhlich soll mein Herze springen*:

> There is just a slight flavour of the monastery and mysticism, but no more than is justified. After all, it is right to speak of 'I' and 'Christ' as well as 'we', and what that means can hardly be expressed better than it is in this hymn.[3]

All his thoughts about those dear to him are constantly turned into prayers of petition, and in the same way he continually begs them to pray for him. 'Let us promise to remain faithful in interceding for each other', he writes to Bethge.[4] And, in one of the last letters, he declares his conviction of how much he owes to the prayerful intercession of 'others, both known and unknown'.[5] He even describes finding consolation and support in making the sign of the cross morning and evening, though this never made him a 'homo religiosus' nor indeed did he ever become one:

> I have found that following Luther's instruction to 'make the sign of the cross' at our morning and evening prayers is in itself helpful. There is something objective about it, and that is what is particularly badly needed here. Don't be alarmed; I shall not come out of here a *homo religiosus*! On the contrary, my fear and distrust of 'religiosity' have become greater than ever here.[6]

Although there is one day when he can say 'it is remarkable how little I miss going to church',[7] there are other days, especially

[3] *Ibid.*, 112.
[4] *Ibid.*, 89.
[5] *Ibid.*, 214.
[6] *Ibid.*, 97.
[7] *Ibid.*, 108.

the great feasts, when he thinks not only of his family, his friends and his fellow-prisoners, but also of 'the Church and its services'.[8] On Pentecost Sunday, 1943, he even celebrates a service by himself, summoning to it in his mind all those he loves:

> When the bells rang this morning, I longed to go to church, but instead I did as John did on the island of Patmos, and had such a splendid service of my own, that I did not feel lonely at all, for you were all with me, every one of you, and so were the congregations in whose company I have kept Whitsuntide.[9]

He wishes he could 'hear a good sermon on Sundays',[10] and complains of not being allowed to have a minister to see him.[11] He regrets not having been able to receive the eucharist with his friend Bethge, and yet realizes that 'we have shared spiritually, although not physically, in the gift of confession, absolution and communion'.[12]

All he can do for the moment is to read and re-read the Bible. Seven months after his arrest, he says, he has read the Old Testament precisely two and a half times. The Biblical texts proposed daily for Protestant believers remained up to the end a kind of beacon for him each day, and he frequently refers to them in his letters. With loving care he composed prayers for his fellow-prisoners.

For he never ceased to be filled with the thought of others. His permanent worry was lest his family and friends should have to undergo the same suffering as himself. He made a point of stressing that it was far from unbearable, despite fits of melancholy which he also spoke of. The word we find perhaps most often of all in his letters is 'thankfulness'.

Bonhoeffer has used the term 'straightforward' to characterize what was at work in him—and it was surely a development—during those long months of captivity.[13] In this perspective too —independent of the background of meditation and prayer we

[8] *Ibid.*, 54.
[9] *Ibid.*, 55.
[10] *Ibid.*, 69.
[11] *Ibid.*, 87.
[12] *Ibid.*, 88.
[13] *Ibid.*, 150.

have been considering—we must now listen as he sets out the major themes of his final, profound reflexions.

The world come of age

At the root of those reflexions lies the certainty that the contemporary world has reached adulthood. The world in which we live, the world to which the Church must give her message, is a world come of age. By this he means a world which does not think itself bound to leave the determining of its fate to anyone outside itself, and which has in fact an ever greater mastery over what used in the past to be called 'the secrets of nature'. 'The movement that began about the thirteenth century', says Bonhoeffer, 'has in our time reached an undoubted completion. Man has learnt to deal with himself in all questions of importance without recourse to the "working hypothesis" called "God".'[14]

When writing this, he had just been studying the work of the physicist Weizsäcker on 'the world view of physics', *Das Weltbild der Physik*. He had noted at the time:

> It has again brought home to me quite clearly how wrong it is to use God as a stop-gap for the incompleteness of our knowledge. If in fact the frontiers of knowledge are being pushed further and further back (and that is bound to be the case), then God is being pushed back with them and is therefore continually in retreat. We are to find God in what we know, not in what we do not know; God wants us to realize his presence, not in unsolved problems but in those that are solved.[15]

Previously, in the *Ethics*, Bonhoeffer had stressed the absolutely new situation brought about by 'the unparallelled rise of technology' in our time: a technology no longer 'in the service of religion, of kings, of art, and of the daily needs of men', but now 'in essence not service but mastery, mastery over nature'. And that technology 'has a soul of its own. Its symbol is the machine.' He pointed out at the same time how 'naïve faith' might well see this as being a demoniacal force, but that whether or no, it is now impossible to move backwards. We must face the fact that 'the

[14] *Ibid.*, 178. [15] *Ibid.*, 174.

age of technology is a genuine heritage of our western history'.[16] And he became gradually more convinced that the evolution which has led to modern science and technology must be marked out as one of the prime objects for Christian consideration.

But it is not only in relation to nature, and because of the advance of science and technology, that the contemporary world has become aware of its adult status, and that God seems to be losing ground. It is also in relation to the great human problems which had previously seemed to mark man's limitations and force him in a sense upon the mercy of someone or something outside himself. Here Bonhoeffer's notes are not so easy to sum up in any one straightforward position. He was undoubtedly struck by the experience of those with whom circumstances had brought him into contact, men who, as a result of the Nazi education (or anti-education) they had had, and of the impossible situations in which the war had placed them, evinced human characteristics which had little in common with the norms instilled into Bonhoeffer the aristocrat. Yet it seemed to him that he could recognize in them elements more in keeping with human nature as it had developed in the present day. What he found most noteworthy was that, upon 'the wider human problems such as guilt, suffering and death', our contemporaries felt no need to turn to God:

> It is now possible to find, even for these questions, human answers that take no account whatever of God. In point of fact, people deal with these questions without God (it has always been so), and it is simply not true to say that only Christianity has the answers to them.[17]

However, in 'the outline of a book I have planned', a little later, Bonhoeffer pointed out that man, though now, with his technology and various forms of organization, largely master of all the forces of nature and of life, still has to face the problem of himself.[18]

Whether these analyses are accurate or only approximate is of less importance than the line of theological thinking Bonhoeffer

[16] *Ethics*, 98-9.
[17] *Letters and Papers from Prison*, 175. [18] *Ibid.*, 208-9.

intended to work out in relation to them. The first idea he stresses is that of the failure, but also the mistaken effort, of the Christian preaching and apologetics that are centred upon the weakness of man.

> Theology has on the one hand resisted this development with apologetics, and has taken up arms—in vain—against Darwinism, etc. On the other hand, it has accommodated itself to the development by restricting God to the so-called ultimate questions as a *deus ex machina*; that means that he becomes the answer to life's problems, and the solution of its needs and conflicts. So if anyone has no such difficulties, or if he refuses to go into these things, to allow others to pity him, then either he cannot open to God; or else he must be shown that he is, in fact, deeply involved in such problems, needs, and conflicts, without admitting or knowing it.[19]

It is easy enough then to call in the assistance of existential philosophy or certain forms of psychiatry. Both 'have worked out some quite ingenious methods in that direction'—that is, in proving to man that happiness is his undoing, health really sickness, vitality nothing but an expression of despair. . . .[20]

We sometimes try, without necessarily having recourse to such stratagems, to soften the dismissal of God from the world of public life by retaining him 'at least in the sphere of the "personal", the "inner", and the "private".'

> The secrets known by a man's valet—that is, to put it crudely, the range of his intimate life, from prayer to his sexual life—have become the hunting ground of modern pastoral workers. In this way they resemble (though with quite different intentions), the dirtiest gutter journalists.[21]

This phenomenon can only be seen as a compensation for an inferiority complex. But it is quite wrong to think that to enable man to face God we must first begin by humiliating him, just as it is equally wrong to try to relegate God solely to the area of the secret and intimate life.

[19] *Ibid.*, 188. [20] *Ibid.*, 188; cf. 174, 190.
[21] *Ibid.*, 191.

> When Jesus blessed sinners, they were real sinners, but Jesus did not make everyone a sinner first. He called them away from their sin, not into their sin. . . . It is true that Jesus cared about people on the fringe of human society, such as harlots and tax-collectors, but never about them alone, for he sought to care about man as such. Never did he question a man's health, vigour, or happiness, regarded in themselves, or regard them as evil fruits; else why should he heal the sick and restore strength to the weak? Jesus claims for himself and the Kingdom of God the whole of human life in all its manifestations.[22]

Bonhoeffer's concern was to have a robust Christianity rather than a Christianity on the defensive, with all the lowering standards, all the dishonesty to which such a position so easily leads. The majesty of God must never be compromised by our fears, our resentments, our search for the easy way out.

> I therefore want to start from the premise that God should not be smuggled into some last secret place, but that we should frankly recognize that the world, and people, have come of age, that we should not run man down in his worldliness, but confront him with God at his strongest point, that we should give up all our clerical tricks, and not regard psychotherapy and existentialist philosophy as God's pioneers. The importunity of all these people is far too unaristocratic for the Word of God to ally itself with them. The Word of God is far removed from this revolt of mistrust, this revolt from below. On the contrary, it reigns.[23]

'Religionless' interpretation of dogma

How is the Word of God to be heard, and how is it to exercise, as it must, its sovereignty on the world at large, which is our world too? Or, better perhaps, how can Christ impress his demands upon it, and take possession of it to enable it to attain to its true goal? These are the questions which Bonhoeffer is trying to answer, or at least to clarify, in his reflexions on a 'religionless' interpretation of the dogmas of faith.

In fact, the world at large, not feeling any need to rely on anyone outside itself, or to seek help elsewhere, must largely be con-

[22] *Ibid.*, 189. [23] *Ibid.*, 193.

sidered an irreligious world. In general only a minority can be said to share the goal of 'religion', or at least of 'religiosity'.

Bonhoeffer himself frequently puts both these terms into quotation marks, evidently meaning that their meaning must be rightly understood. He has nowhere defined them very precisely. However we find some indications of the kind of thing he intended. He asks, for instance: 'How do we speak of God—without religion, i.e. without the temporally conditioned presuppositions of metaphysics, inwardness, and so on?'[24] Religion is obviously that special sphere which man reserves for a God situated essentially in another world, whichever side it lies of the concrete reality where we are living and creating. The God of 'metaphysics' is basically the God of the deists: the great architect of the universe who presents us with a ready-made 'nature', and for whom man is in one sense no more than a toy. The God of 'inwardness', is the God of a certain fashionable Methodist pietism, and can only be sought by withdrawing as far as possible from the activity and the realities of the world. Thus 'religion' always appears in the guise of man's escaping from himself, or at least trying to evade reality.

The next question is whether the link which has for so long existed between Christianity and religion is a necessary one, and if not, what can faith mean to man in his new, 'religionless' state. Bonhoeffer puts this, giving a few new twists to the idea of 'religion', but in such a way as ultimately to lead us back to the same basic ideas we have just been considering.

> What is bothering me incessantly is the question what Christianity really is, or indeed who Christ really is, for us today. The time when people could be told everything by means of words, whether theological or pious, is over, and so is the time of inwardness and conscience—and that means the time of religion in general. We are moving towards a completely religionless time; people as they are now simply cannot be religious any more. Even those who honestly describe themselves as 'religious' do not in the least act up to it, and so they presumably mean something quite different by 'religious'.[25]

[24] *Ibid.*, 153. [25] *Ibid.*, 152.

In such a situation, it is pointless to try to continue as in the past nineteen centuries, to form our preaching and our theology upon the 'religious *a priori*' of man. We shall certainly come to see this as having been a contingent and transitory element in human nature. The temptation then to be avoided above all others is that of seizing upon a few 'last survivals of the age of chivalry', or a few less intellectually honest men, as offering us that 'religious' basis that is not to be found among mankind as a whole. Still less 'are we to fall upon a few unfortunate people in their hour of need and exercise a sort of religious compulsion on them?' The only question for us must be to know how Christ can 'become the Lord of the religionless as well'.[26]

Bonhoeffer realized that he was not the first to see the problem of faith and the problem of Revelation in relation to religion. Karl Barth in particular had devoted a whole section of his *Church Dogmatics* to it. But Bonhoeffer did not consider that Barth really carried his insights to their logical conclusion. He 'has arrived at a positivism of revelation which has nevertheless remained essentially a restoration'. As for Bultmann, and his 'de-mythologizing', Bonhoeffer's view was not that he went 'too far', but that 'he did not go far enough': more precisely, he put the problem inaccurately, and dealt with it with the tools of an outmoded form of criticism.

> It is not only the 'mythological' concepts, such as miracle, ascension, and so on (which are not in principle separable from the concepts of God, faith, etc.), but 'religious' concepts generally, which are problematic. You cannot, as Bultmann supposes, separate God and miracle, but you must be able to interpret and proclaim *both* in a 'non-religious' sense. Bultmann's approach is fundamentally still a liberal one (i.e. abridging the gospel), whereas I am trying to think theologically.[27]

On this more profound, theological level, Bonhoeffer questions whether it would not be true to say of 'religion' what Paul says of circumcision, namely that it is not a necessary condition for salvation. He considers too that faith as defined in the Old and

[26] *Ibid.*, 153. [27] *Ibid.*, 156; cf. 177 ff.

New Testaments does not relate to a religion of deliverance and redemption similar to those we also find elsewhere in the ancient East. The liberation and deliverance it does incidentally include are, unlike those of the redemption myths, effected by a return first of all to this world and its work.[28] Furthermore, Jesus was not a 'homo religiosus', but a *man* in the fullest sense of the word.[29] Nor was Christ simply 'an object of religion', but something quite different, 'really the Lord of the world'.[30] Similarly, whereas 'the religious act is always something partial, faith is always something whole, involving the whole of one's life'.[31]

The powerlessness of God

One theme comes, in the letters from prison, to complement the idea of the world come of age, and the 'religionless' interpretation of the dogmas of faith : that of the powerlessness, or suffering, of God. More accurately, this theme seems to Bonhoeffer to provide the beginning of a solution to the problems he is considering. For an honest recognition of the situation we have been describing must not lead us to abandon all attempts to bear witness to Christ. It can even help us to see, in a new light, some essential aspects of the Gospel. When all is said and done, the religious crisis our age is living through makes it possible to clarify our true situation in relation to God, and in doing so to have a better understanding of his mysterious plans.

> So our coming of age leads us to a true recognition of our situation before God. God would have us know that we must live as men who manage our lives without him. The God who is with us is the God who forsakes us (Mark 15 :34). The God who lets us live in the world without the working hypothesis of God is the God before whom we stand continually. Before God and with God we live without God. God lets himself be pushed out of the world on to the cross. He is weak and powerless in the world, and that is precisely the way, the only way, in which he is with us and helps

[28] *Ibid.*, 181-85.
[29] *Ibid.*, 201.
[30] *Ibid.*, 153-4.
[31] *Ibid.*, 199; cf. 153-4, 195-6.

us. Matt. 8 :17 makes it quite clear that Christ helps us, not by virtue of his omnipotence, but by virtue of his weakness and suffering.[32]

From this viewpoint, the attitude of faith required of us, like the revelation we are given of God, is fundamentally different from—and indeed the absolute opposite of—the attitude and ideas which generally characterize 'religion'.

Here is the decisive difference between Christianity and all religions. Man's religiosity makes him look in his distress to the power of God in the world; God is the *deus ex machina*. The Bible directs man to God's powerlessness and suffering; only the suffering God can help. To that extent we may say that the development towards the world's coming of age outlined above, which has done away with a false conception of God, opens up a way of seeing the God of the Bible, who wins power and space in the world by his weakness. This will probably be the starting-point for our 'secular interpretation'.[33]

That interpretation is based upon a paradox which it simultaneously makes clear to us: the paradox of the justification of the sinner.

When we speak of God in a 'non-religious' way, we just speak of him in such a way that the godlessness of the world is not in some way concealed, but rather revealed, and thus exposed to an unexpected light. The world that has come of age is more godless, and perhaps for that very reason nearer to God, than the world before its coming of age.[34]

While pondering this, Bonhoeffer was also working on a short poem, 'Christians and Pagans', which is an attempt to express the same idea:

Men go to God when they are sore bestead,
Pray to him for succour, for his peace, for bread,
For mercy for the sick, sinning or dead;
All men do so, Christian and unbelieving.

Men go to God when he is sore bestead,
Find him poor and scorned, without shelter or bread,

[32] *Ibid.*, 196. [33] *Ibid.*, 196-7.
[34] *Ibid.*, 200.

Whelmed under weight of the wicked, the weak, the dead:
Christians stand by God in his hour of grieving.

God goeth to every man when sore bestead,
Feedeth body and spirit with his bread,
For Christians, pagans alike he hangeth dead:
And both alike forgiving.[35]

The dissolution of Christianity?

It seems to me that this poem, like the paradoxes which emerge from the preceding quotations, have their place in the great framework of Christian mysticism—which so often gives us just this same sense of being at sea, being out of our depth. This inspiration, mystical in the best sense of the word, is particularly striking in these 'disturbing' thoughts of the last letters. In them Bonhoeffer expresses more than simply the conclusions which must flow from certain objective statements, or even the results of bold thinking: he is expressing his own inner experience to a close friend.

> I discovered later, and am still discovering right up to this moment, that it is only by living completely in this world that one learns to have faith. One must completely abandon any attempt to make something of oneself, whether it be a saint, or a converted sinner, or a churchman (a so-called priestly type!), a righteous man or an unrighteous one, a sick man or a healthy one. By this-worldliness I mean living unreservedly in life's duties, problems, successes and failures, experiences and perplexities. In so doing we throw ourselves completely into the arms of God, taking seriously, not our own sufferings, but those of God in the world—watching with Christ in Gethsemane. That, I think, is faith, that is *metanoia*; and that is how one becomes a man and a Christian (cf. Jer. 45!). How can success make us arrogant, or failure lead us astray, when we share in God's sufferings through a life of this kind?[36]

And he goes on to indicate the intimate nature of this confidence:

[35] *Ibid.* [36] *Ibid.*, 201-2.

I think you see what I mean, even though I put it so briefly. I am glad to have been able to learn this, and I know I have been able to do so only along the road that I have travelled. So I am grateful for the past and the present, and content with them. You may be surprised at such a personal letter; but if for once I want to say this kind of thing, whom should I say it to? May God in his mercy lead us through these times; but above all may he lead us to himself.[37]

We know, however, that mystical ideas carry their own danger; future generations are all too likely to seize upon them and distort them into mistaken or destructive theories. Furthermore, it may legitimately be wondered whether, in the words I have just quoted, Bonhoeffer is not falling into the very pietism he so wants to avoid, by putting forward one of the most suspect expressions of 'religion'.

What is quite clear is the very positive nature of his concern and of what he says. As we have already seen, throughout all his penetrating self-questioning, he is endeavouring to discover 'How can Christ become the Lord of the religionless as well?'[38] The Church must be helped to carry out its mission by coming out of its 'stagnation', by moving out 'again into the open air of intellectual discussion with the world'.[39] It is not a matter of polemics and apologetics, but of understanding the 'adulthood of the world'—'better than it understands itself, namely on the basis of the Gospel, and in the light of Christ'.[40]

Though we cannot doubt his good will, do his expressions and the conclusions that have been drawn from them call for criticism? It would be blind to deny absolutely that they do. I am quite sure that, *as they are expressed*, Bonhoeffer's ideas are not merely disturbing, but actually dangerous. The use that has all too often been made of them shows that I am right in thinking so. It is a fact that, in recent years, they have several times been used as a

[37] *Ibid.*, 202.
[38] *Ibid.*, 153. The mistake for which Bonhoeffer blames Karl Barth and his 'positivist doctrine of revelation' is that by it 'the world is made to depend on itself and left to its own devices' (*ibid.*, 157).
[39] *Ibid.*, 208. [40] *Ibid.*, 177-182.

basis for considering the 'adult world' and the distinction between faith and religion in such a way that Christianity and the Church come to be seen as only truly fulfilled by being abolished altogether. Thus, in his scholarly work on Bonhoeffer, *Von der Kirche zur Welt* (From the Church to the World),[41] the east German theologian, Hanfried Müller, uses them to prove that, in the mind of the 'final', in other words of the only genuine, Bonhoeffer, the Church can be truly fulfilled only by participating in the construction of socialism.

Yet, even aside from what we have shown here of the existing atmosphere, and of the presuppositions of traditional faith within which we must situate Bonhoeffer's bold explorations, he himself constantly insisted on the unfinished and one-sided nature of his reflexions. After outlining them to Bethge, he writes:

> Forgive me for writing all this in German script; normally I do this only when my writing is for my own use—and perhaps what I have written was more to clear my own mind than to edify you.[42]

He realized better than anyone that he was only putting out feelers for research that must be followed up:

> Sometimes I am quite shocked at what I say, especially in the first part, which is mainly critical; and so I am looking forward to getting to the more constructive part. But the whole thing has been so little discussed that it often sounds clumsy. In any case, it can't be printed yet, and it will have to go through the 'purifier' later on.[43]

Indeed, his thoughts are very often put in the form of questions. He certainly saw himself as posing problems, quite as much as, if not more than, supporting theses. In regard to the 'non-religious interpretation' he is working for, 'the job is too big for me to finish just yet'.[44] He admits to the absence of clarity in much of his thinking:

> But it is all very much in the early stages; and, as usual, I am

[41] H. Müller, *Von der Kirche zur Welt*, Hamburg, 1961.
[42] *Letters and Papers from Prison*, 157; cf. 177.
[43] *Ibid.*, 215. [44] *Ibid.*, 195.

being led on more by an instinctive feeling for questions that will arise later than by any conclusions that I have already reached about them.[45]

When Bethge asks his permission to show some of his letters to other people, his reply is:

> If you want of your own accord to send . . . extracts from my letters, you can, of course, do so. I would not do it myself as yet, because you are the only person with whom I venture to think aloud, as it were, in the hope of clarifying my thoughts.[46]

He is well aware that many problems, among them some of the most essential ones, remain to be solved:

> The questions to be answered would surely be: What do a church, a community, a sermon, a liturgy, a Christian life mean in a religionless world? How do we speak of God—without religion. . . ?[47]

A few months later, in his 'Outline for a book', he rests content with a few notes:

> What do we really believe? I mean, believe in such a way that we stake our lives on it? The problem of the Apostles' Creed? 'What *must* I believe?' is the wrong question; antiquated controversies, especially those between the different sects; the Lutheran versus Reformed, and to some extent the Roman Catholic versus Protestant . . . no longer carry conviction. . . . Barth and the Confessing Church have encouraged us to entrench ourselves persistently behind the 'faith of the Church', and evade the honest question as to what we ourselves really believe.

As for the Church:

> The Church is the Church only when it exists for others. To make a start, it should give away all its property to those in need. The clergy must live solely of the free-will offerings of their congregations, or possibly engage in some secular calling. The Church must share in the secular problems of ordinary human life, not dominating, but helping and serving.

Then, thinking in particular of the situation in Germany at the

[45] *Ibid.*, 177-8.
[46] *Ibid.*, 193.
[47] *Ibid.*, 153.

time, he stresses the part the Church must play in defending fundamental human values, for instance through preaching:

> The question of revising the creeds (the Apostles' Creed); revision of Christian apologetics; reform of the training for the ministry and the pattern of clerical life.

He concludes:

> All this is very crude and condensed, but there are certain things that I am anxious to say simply and clearly—things that we so often shirk. Whether I shall succeed is another matter, especially if I cannot discuss it with you. I hope it may be of some help for the Church's future.[48]

It is doubly to be regretted that Bonhoeffer had time to do no more than point out all these problems: first, because they are problems which in fact preoccupy a great many Christians today, and Bonhoeffer would undoubtedly have brought much light to bear upon them with his free and vigorous faith; and second, because he would certainly have blocked the road along which some of his more heedless readers were to stray, the road of resolving questions out of hand by simply suppressing them.

And Bonhoeffer did in fact foresee such *simpliste* interpretations of his thinking. This is clear from what he has to say of people who are aware only of what may be called the horizontal dimension of life:

> I have long had a special affection for the season between Easter and Ascension day. Here is another great tension. How can men stand earthly tensions if they know nothing of the tension between earth and heaven?[49]

He writes, admittedly, that 'Our relation to God is not a "religious" relationship to the highest, most powerful, and best Being imaginable—that is not authentic transcendence—but our relation to God is a new life in "existence for others",' a life in conformity with Jesus's own being.[50] He also lays stress on the idea that 'the transcendental is not infinite and unattainable tasks, but the

[48] *Ibid.*, 208-11. [49] *Ibid.*, 148.
[50] *Ibid.*, 210.

neighbour who is within reach',[51] the transcendent is present in what is temporal and immanent. But he also makes it clear that he does not mean by this 'the shallow and banal this-worldliness of the enlightened, the comfortable, or the lascivious, but the profound this-worldliness, characterized by discipline and the constant knowledge of death and resurrection'.[52] He supports the statement that 'God makes use of us in his dealings with other people', but makes it equally clear that this must not 'lead to an unrealistic cult of the human'.[53] And in the *Ethics* he foresees and warns against the illusion of those who think Christianity can be reduced simply to an attitude of charity, taking out of it everything that belongs specifically to faith, every reference to the transcendence of God:

> Only he who knows God knows what love is; it is not the other way round; it is not that we first of all by nature know what love is and therefore know also what God is. No one knows God unless God reveals Himself to him. . . . There is given no general definition of love, in the sense, for example, of its being the laying down of one's life for others. . . . Love is inseparably bound up with the name of Jesus Christ as the revelation of God. . . . Love, therefore, is not man's choice, but is the election of man by God.[54]

He knows that *The Cost of Discipleship* represents a line of thought that is not without danger: the danger of pursuing holiness for its own sake. But though he recognizes that danger more clearly now, he states in so many words that he does not want to take back anything he wrote then.[55] 'I have certainly learnt a great deal', he writes from prison, 'but I don't think I have changed very much. . . . Self-development is, of course, an entirely different matter.'[56] He was too deeply convinced of the value of

[51] *Ibid.* [52] *Ibid.*, 201.
[53] *Ibid.*, 212. [54] *Ethics*, 50-52.
[55] *Letters and Papers from Prison*, 201.
[56] *Ibid.*, 149. Bethge, who probably knew him better than anyone else, considers that we shall undoubtedly come more and more to see 'how the late Bonhoeffer grew out of the early' (*Die mündige Welt.*, II, 5).

continuity,[57] and of his own inheritance, to want simply to jettison realities which, in some of their forms, seemed to him to have been brought into question by the new situation which he saw presenting itself at the end of his life.

As we have seen, the liberal principle of reduction, as applied for instance by Bultmann, seemed to him inadmissible. The difficult route he was trying to pick out, and which he did not have the time to pursue, was by his own admission a 'theological' one, avoiding the pitfalls of a liberalism which made things too easy by simply getting rid of difficulties, a Methodist form of pietism which could become lost in the 'inwardness' of 'religion', and an ecclesiastical 'positivism' concerning Revelation, which allowed of no recognition of the different 'levels' of truth, nor the different conditions under which it was received.

Though Bonhoeffer was not able to explore fully a road which he managed only to glimpse from his imprisonment, he has left us certain reflexions which, though apparently unrelated to the problems mentioned up to now, are in fact useful in guiding the researches of those who have come after him. The first collection of notes we shall look at deals with 'shame', and a return to the idea that governed the ancient discipline of the secret. These reflexions make it possible to see not only the outlines of his own intellectual temperament, but also the positive values which Bonhoeffer was setting out to defend. The second collection relates to the distinction and also the relationship between the 'ultimate' and the 'penultimate' things—a theme which leads us to the heart of his understanding of faith.

Shame and the discipline of the secret

In the *Ethics*, Bonhoeffer analyses the meaning of shame, which bears witness to the fact that man's original unity with God and his fellow-man has been destroyed (cf. Gen 3 : 7), but which also shows that even our bodies have their own freedom.[58]

[57] Cf. *Letters and Papers from Prison*, 123-4; *Ethics*, 106 ff.
[58] Cf. *Ethics*, 20 ff.

In his prison letters, he mentions several times his distaste for those who are unable to conceal their fear but make a public show of it, thus displaying the poverty of people without any inner discipline, without any 'mystery'. For himself, when in danger, he prefers to seek support in the privacy of prayer—all the more so since at such times he finds it impossible to offer others 'any Christian encouragement or comfort'. Indeed it seems to him 'wrong' to 'force religion down [anyone's] throat just then'. He has the liveliest awareness of the respect we should have for the mystery of the fundamental realities of man, as well as of God. We have already seen this in the letters he wrote during the war to the families of 'brothers' who had been killed. After being visited by some people who had been bombed out, he notes in a letter:

> But I am afraid I am bad at comforting; I can listen all right, but I can hardly find anything to say. But perhaps the way one asks about some things and not about others help to suggest what really matters; and it seems to me more important actually to share someone's distress than to use smooth words about it. I have no sympathy with some wrong-headed attempts to explain away distress, because instead of being a comfort, they are the exact opposite. So I do not try to explain it, and I think this is the right way to begin, although it is only a beginning, and I very seldom get beyond it. I sometimes think that real comfort must break in just as unexpectedly as the distress. But I admit that that may be a subterfuge.[59]

Just as he is anxious not to violate the mystery of suffering by offering false palliatives, so he feels a spontaneous dislike for bringing in the name of God when talking to people who use it lightly, or in an ambiguous sense.

> I often ask myself why a 'Christian instinct' often draws me more to the religionless people than to the religious, by which I do not in the least mean with any evangelizing intention, but, I might almost say, 'in brotherhood'. While I am often reluctant to mention God by name to religious people—because that name somehow seems to me here not to ring true and I feel myself to be slightly dishonest (it is particularly bad when others start to talk

[59] *Letters and Papers from Prison*, 124-5.

in religious jargon; I then dry up almost completely and feel awkward and uncomfortable)—to people with no religion I can on occasion mention him by name quite calmly and as a matter of course.[60]

And it is during his reflexions on the religionless world that he twice recalls the ancient ecclesiastical discipline of the secret, whereby the realities of the faith were communicated only at the end of an initiation period. This, he thought, might well become relevant in a new form in our own day. For it is always essential that 'the *mysteries* of the Christian faith are protected against profanation'.[61]

In other words, the way to a 'religionless' interpretation of the Biblical tradition which seems to Bonhoeffer to be a necessity for a 'world come of age', must not, to his way of thinking, be sought through a two-dimensional naturalism, a rootless humanism, or a philanthropy that denies the mystery of human nature. Far from resulting in the dissolution of the proper object of faith, far from allowing it to be diminished or distorted, it should lead to a new appreciation of the transcendent reality upon which that faith as a whole depends, and upon which it is constantly nourished. We are bound not merely to become open to a world which we have to accept for what it is, just as has God himself, but also to seek genuine recollection—not the recollection of escape, but of penetrating beyond the appearances to the very heart of this mystery of creation and reconciliation upon which everything else rests. As Bonhoeffer explains in the *Ethics*, just as the Church needs a certain 'space' simply to be (though not in the sense of trying 'to deprive the world of a piece of its territory'),[62] so, too, faith demands a certain interiority—but one which has nothing in common with the false interiority of some kinds of religiosity, for unlike them, it enables us to be more profoundly present in the world, more respectful of its autonomy, and of what can only be called its mysteries.

This indispensable recollection, combined with a practical

[60] *Ibid.*, 154.
[61] *Ibid.*, 157. Italics are the author's.
[62] *Ethics*, 201-2.

dedication is the major characteristic of the Christian life as Bonhoeffer envisages it in this new age he tries to describe:

> Our being Christian today will be limited to two things: prayer and righteous action among men. All Christian thinking, speaking, and organizing must be born anew out of this prayer and action. . . . The Christian cause will be a silent affair, but there will be those who pray and do right and wait for God's own time.[63]

For himself, he knows how large a place prayer must occupy at the very centre of his bold thinking:

> It is only in the spirit of prayer that any such work can be begun and carried through.[64]

The 'ultimate' and 'penultimate' things

Bonhoeffer himself relates the notion of a discipline of the secret with another theme he has much to say about—the 'ultimate' and 'penultimate' things.[65] His notes and reflexions on this point gives us what is perhaps the best perspective in which to understand his ideas, the best context in which to see his bold, and at first sight somewhat disconcerting, schemata in their true light.

It is his idea that Christian faith, which is the response to a revelation and a salvation effected in time and in the flesh, is only genuine to the extent that it remains rooted in this world. It gains nothing—it is rather emptied of substance—by trying to break its links with what makes it at once realistic and something special. Though it is true that God is not to be confused with the reality of the world, and that he awaits us at a point beyond all our human plans and interests, it is equally true that it is in this earthly reality, within our own human history, that he comes to us and wants us to recognize him.

> I believe we ought so to love and trust God in our *lives*, and in all the good things that he sends us, that when the time comes

[63] *Letters and Papers from Prison*, 172.
[64] *Ibid.*, 208. [65] *Ibid.*, 154.

(but not before!) we may go to him with love, trust, and joy. But, to put it plainly, for a man in his wife's arms to be hankering after the world is, in mild terms, a piece of bad taste, and not God's will. We ought to find and love God in what he actually gives us; if it pleases him to allow us to enjoy some overwhelmingly earthly happiness, we must not try to be more pious than God himself and allow our happiness to be corrupted by presumption and arrogance, and by unbridled religious fantasy which is never satisfied with what God gives. God will see to it that the man who finds him in his earthly happiness and thanks him for it does not lack reminder that earthly things are transient. . . . But everything has its time, and the main thing is that we keep step with God, and not keep pressing on a few steps ahead—nor keep dawdling a step behind.[66]

The 'ultimate things' are in God's hand. They are the work of his Word and his grace. Bonhoeffer explains this in an important section of the *Ethics*.[67] The 'ultimate' character of the saving Word of God must be understood in two ways. First, 'qualitatively': it is impossible to get any further; this is indeed 'the last word' which judges all things and is judged by none. But it must also be understood in a 'temporal' sense: the 'ultimate' reality is always preceded by a 'penultimate', an endeavour, a suffering, a supplication, a hope, whose conclusion it is. One cannot grasp the 'ultimate' character of God's word nor say anything about it, unless one recognizes the place of the 'penultimate' realities.

Bonhoeffer uses these categories, taken from the temporal sphere, to express what in classical theology is called the relationship between the natural and the supernatural. The section of the *Ethics* which deals with them comes immediately before one devoted to working out the ways of showing the importance of the concept of 'the natural' in Christian ethics. The interest of the categories he has chosen lies in the fact that they are always relative to one another, even though it remains true that, in the last analysis, it is upon the 'ultimate' that everything else depends. For Bonhoeffer, the disadvantage of the 'spatial thinking' suggested by the natural-supernatural relationship, is that it does not

[66] *Ibid.*, 111. [67] *Ethics*, 120 ff.

make clear the dynamic connection between the two, the continual passing of the one into the other, which is reality itself, and takes effect in 'the unique reality of Christ'.

The connection between the 'ultimate' and the 'penultimate' corresponds to a basic structure of the Christian faith, a structure given to us first in Revelation. It is the connection between the Old and the New Testaments. Like Luther, like most of the medieval theologians, like the early Fathers, and above all like the New Testament writers themselves, Bonhoeffer recognizes clearly that the understanding of faith must always be linked with the understanding of that connection.[68]

During his imprisonment he became more and more convinced of the major and indeed indispensable part played by the Old Testament in Christian faith as such: it prevents that faith becoming empty of content, of drifting off into splendid thoughts or empty words, of turning into cheap pietism.

> My thoughts and feelings seem to be getting more and more like those of the Old Testament, and in recent months I have been reading the Old Testament much more than the New. It is only when one knows the unutterability of the name of God that one can utter the name of Jesus Christ; it is only when one loves life and the earth so much that without them everything seems to be over that one can believe in the resurrection and a new world; it is only when one submits to God's law that one can speak of grace. . . . In my opinion it is not Christian to want to take our thoughts and feelings too quickly and too directly from the New Testament. . . . One cannot and must not speak the last word before the last but one. We live in the last but one and believe the last, don't we?[69]

It is in conformity with this structuring of revelation and faith that Bonhoeffer tries to find God not so much at the boundaries of reality as at its heart:

> I should like to speak of God not on the boundaries but at the centre, not in weakness but in strength; and therefore not in

[68] For the tradition on this subject see H. de Lubac, *Histoire et Esprit*, Paris, 1950, and *Exégèse médiévale, Paris*, 1959-64.

[69] *Letters and Papers from Prison*, 103-4.

death and guilt but in man's life and goodness.[70] As to the boundaries, it seems to me better to be silent and leave the insoluble unsolved. Belief in the resurrection is *not* the 'solution' of the problem of death. God's 'beyond' is not the beyond of our cognitive faculties. The transcendence of epistemological theory has nothing to do with the transcendence of God. God is beyond in the midst of our life. The Church stands, not at the boundaries where human powers give out, but in the middle of village. That is how it is in the Old Testament, and in this sense we still read the New Testament far too little in the light of the Old.[71]

However, it is primarily in Jesus Christ that the necessary tension between the last and next-to-last things is ultimately expressed and resolved. After all, it is in him that there takes place that fulfilment and transfiguration of the Old Testament in the New, which *is* Christian revelation, which *is* salvation. It is in him, in his liberated and risen body, that there took place once and for all, and still continues to take place, the movement of God's eternity into the world's time, and the world's time into God's eternity. And it is also to him, to Jesus Christ precisely as man, and as crucified and risen, that Bonhoeffer refers in the *Ethics* in order to express the right relationship between the 'ultimate' and the 'penultimate', which is, let me say once more, the genuine structure of faith.

Just as we have seen how he stresses the reciprocity existing between these 'ultimate' and 'penultimate' things, and warns us not to try to dissociate them, so too he stresses here the importance of never separating the three 'moments' of which Christ's work is made manifest—the incarnation, the cross and the resurrection. It is all the more important to be very clear about this, because what he has to say about the suffering and the powerlessness of God might well lead us to think that his only purpose is to

[70] In the *Ethics*, Bonhoeffer points out that we must not only consider Jesus's dealings with the wicked, but also with the good (60-63).

[71] *Letters and Papers from Prison*, 155. Again, he writes in regard to the two Testaments: 'The only difference between the two Testaments in this respect is that in the Old the blessing includes the cross, and in the New the cross includes the blessing' (*ibid.*, 206-7). In a paper written in 1936, he had explained how the only true Church must always be rooted in the Old Testament (*G.S.*, III, 328; *The Way to Freedom*, 46).

reformulate that 'theology of the cross' which some forms of Protestantism are strongly tempted to make the whole of their teaching, and which can be used to justify the most lamentable inactivity.

> In Jesus Christ we have faith in the incarnate, crucified and risen God. In the incarnation we learn of the love of God for his creation;[72] in the crucifixion we learn of the judgment of God upon all flesh; and in the resurrection we learn of God's will for a new world. There could be no greater error than to tear these three elements apart; for each of them comprises the whole. . . . We have tried to make clear the unity and the diversity of the incarnation, the cross and the resurrection.[73]

Similarly, a Christian life not founded at once on all three realities, not allowing them to express each its own truth and at the same time their indissociable unity, would not be in conformity with the most essential object and most fundamental structures of faith.[74]

In this regard we may note the absolute assurance with which Bonhoeffer witnesses from prison to his faith in the resurrection of Christ. Thus in a letter of Easter greetings in 1944:

> Easter? We are paying more attention to dying than to death. We are more concerned to get over the act of dying than to overcome death. Socrates mastered the art of dying, Christ overcame death as 'the last enemy' (1 Cor. 15:26). There is a real difference between the two things; the one is within the scope of human possibilities, the other means resurrection. It is not from *ars moriendi*, the art of dying, but from the resurrection of Christ, that a new and purifying wind can blow through our present world. *Here* is the answer to *dos moi pou stō kai kinēsō tēn gēn* (give me a place to stand, and I will move the earth). If a few people really believed that and acted on it in their daily lives, a great deal would be changed. To live in the light of the

[72] The incarnation in itself, indeed, manifests both God's acceptance of the concrete reality of mankind and his judgment: 'Jesus was man "without sin" (Heb 4:15); that is what is decisive. Yet among men Jesus lived in the most utter poverty, unmarried, and he died as a criminal. Thus the manhood of Jesus implies already a twofold condemnation of man, the absolute condemnation of sin and the relative condemnation of the established human orders' (*Ethics*, 131).

[73] *Ibid.*, 130-2. [74] *Ibid.*, 130-3.

resurrection—that is what Easter means. Do you find, too, that most people do not know what they really live by?[75]

The cantus firmus

I have spoken earlier of the 'pluridimensional' character which must, it seemed to Bonhoeffer, mark any human life worthy of the name.[76] He likes to compare such a life, and more specifically a genuinely Christian life, to a symphony, with the love of God and his heaven fulfilling the part of the *cantus firmus* above which the voices of this world weave their counterpoint.

> God wants us to love him eternally with our whole hearts—not in such a way as to injure or weaken our earthly love, but to provide a kind of *cantus firmus* to which the other melodies of life provide the counterpoint. One of these contrapuntal themes (which have their own complete independence but are yet related to the *cantus firmus*) is earthly affection. Even in the Bible we have the Song of Songs;[77] and really one can imagine no more ardent, passionate, sensual love than is portrayed there (cf. 7 : 6). . . .[78]

Like the 'ultimate' and 'penultimate' things, the *cantus firmus* and the counterpoint must always be distinguished, and yet at the same time seen in relation to one another :

> Where the *cantus firmus* is clear and plain, the counterpoint can be developed to its limits. The two are 'undivided and yet distinct', in the words of the Chalcedonian Definition, like Christ in his divine and human natures. May not the attraction and importance of polyphony in music consist in its being a musical reflection of this Christological fact and therefore of our *vita christiana*? . . . I wanted to tell you to have a good, clear *cantus firmus*; that is the only way to a full and perfect sound, when the counterpoint has a firm support and cannot come adrift or get out of tune, while remaining a distinct whole in its own right. Only a polyphony of this kind can give a life a wholeness and at the same time assure us that nothing calamitous can happen as long as the *cantus firmus* is kept going.[79]

[75] *Letters and Papers from Prison*, 146.
[76] Cf. *supra*, p.
[77] In reference to the Song of Songs, he wrote on another occasion : 'I must say I should prefer to read it as an ordinary love song, and that is probably the best Christological exposition.' (*Letters and Papers from Prison*, 176).
[78] *Ibid.*, 162. [79] *Ibid.*, 162-3.

The love of God expressed in the *cantus firmus* is concretized for Bonhoeffer in the love of Jesus Christ. It is to that love that we must keep referring to understand his final great ideas, even where he did not manage to formulate them fully or finally, nor, as he himself admitted, to express adequately even the amount he did have time to write. I certainly do not want it to be thought that I do not take the major problems he puts with the utmost seriousness, or that I have any intention of suggesting that they are banal or insubstantial. On the contrary, I trust that by showing the profound faith and genuine piety of their author, I have given them their full weight. I am convinced, however, that we cannot sum them up in a few simple slogans. Nothing is ever easy, nothing cheap, with Bonhoeffer. What I have tried to do is to put these problems back into the deeper context in which they belong, and so cast more light on their significance. And there can be no doubt that that context brings us back to the figure of Christ, who attracted and guided Bonhoeffer at all times. It is that figure who constitutes his firmest point of reference, who assures his most unshakeable convictions, right up to the time of his last letters of all.

> I am still thinking about the assertion . . . that a man cannot live without hope, and that men who have really lost all hope often become wild and wicked. It may be an open question whether in this case hope = illusion. The importance of illusion to one's life should certainly not be underestimated; but for a Christian there must be hope based on a firm foundation. And if even illusion has so much power in people's lives that it can keep life moving, how great a power there is in a hope that is based on certainty, and how invincible a life with such a hope is. 'Christ our hope'—this Pauline formula is the strength of our lives.[80]

He longs to find once more the force of Jesus's own words:

> It is not for us to prophesy the day (though the day will come) when men will once more be called so to utter the word of God that the world will be changed and renewed by it. It will be a new language, perhaps quite non-religious, but liberating and

[80] *Ibid.*, 204.

redeeming—as was Jesus's language; it will shock people and yet overcome them by its power.[81]

In one of the last letters we have, Bonhoeffer once more reaffirms his immovable attachment to Jesus Christ, the principle of all his thinking, the force and light of his whole life:

> If we are to learn what God promises, and what he fulfils, we must persevere in quiet meditation on the life, sayings, deeds, sufferings, and death of Jesus. It is certain that we may always live close to God and in the light of his presence, and that such living is entirely new life for us; that nothing is then impossible for us, because all things are possible with God; that no earthly power can touch us without his will, and that danger and distress can only drive us closer to him. It is certain that we can claim nothing for ourselves, and may yet pray for everything; it is certain that our joy is hidden in suffering and our life in death; it is certain that in all this we are in a fellowship that sustains us. In Jesus God has said his Yes and Amen to it all, and that Yes and Amen is the firm ground on which we stand.[82]

When we talk of the 'meaning' of life, he explains, we are expressing in this non-Biblical term what the Bible means when it speaks of the 'promise'. And it is true that Jesus Christ, the bearer and fulfiller of all God's promises, is also the only being who gives meaning to our lives.

> If this earth was good enough for the man Jesus Christ, if such a man as Jesus lived, then, and only then, has life a meaning for us. If Jesus had not lived, then our life would be meaningless, in spite of all the other people whom we know and honour and love.[83]

Like St Paul, he considers that the only thing that matters is to be 'in him': 'All that we may rightly expect from God, and ask him for, is to be found in Jesus Christ.'[84]

It was Jesus Christ, through all the vicissitudes of his life, through all the gropings of his thought, upon whom Bonhoeffer steadily fixed his gaze. And it was his witness alone that he himself wanted to be among his brothers.

[81] *Ibid.*, 172.
[82] *Ibid.*, 214.
[83] *Ibid.*
[84] *Ibid.*, 213.

Epilogue

Epilogue

I HAVE written this book in the hope of making the man and his ideas better known, for, though no one denies their importance, their significance is for the most part very inadequately understood.

I have tried not to interpose myself between the reader and the subject, though of course even the choice of texts, and the themes singled out for emphasis must involve a certain interpretation. What must be true of any reconstitution of the past is even more true when it concerns a work which could be no more than the beginnings of an outline on many points, and especially when it is one of such amazing richness and variety as to defy systematization. One can only sum it up from a certain point of view. My interpretation may therefore be challenged, and indeed my greatest hope is that it may give rise to a discussion that will bring to light fresh aspects of the inheritance Bonhoeffer has left us.

Furthermore, I have made a point of not setting out to criticize any of his different positions: this is not because I do not think they can be criticized; but because the questions I have touched upon in this book are so many and so important that it would call for another large book to give them any serious critical discussion. It has seemed to me better to begin by simply receiving—with the utmost possible openness and sympathy—a message which certainly has a lot to say to us.

It is a message which concerns all Christians, reaching beyond, or cutting through, differences of Church allegiance. As we have seen, Bonhoeffer saw no reason to gloss over those differences, despite his intransigence in matters of truth. But he was equally convinced, and rightly so, that the Christian conscience is today faced with problems far more serious than any of those upon which the different Christian bodies are divided.

It is true that Bonhoeffer appreciated some of the values most closely linked with the Catholic tradition: not only the sense of a visible Church and the blessings of life in community, but also the sense of a faith rooted in the 'penultimate' realities of nature and history. Yet the Church to which he remained passionately attached throughout his life was primarily the Protestant Church, which meant for him a Church striving to live by the gospel alone. And he felt keenly the danger endemic in Catholicism of trying to re-establish the life of the old law, or of 'naturalizing' the truths of faith. Though we do not necessarily subscribe to his picture of our Church, we have much to gain by acting upon his reminders and warnings.

Throughout the dialogue to which he calls us from time to time the basic problems he puts—those arising out of the modern world in which Christians live and must bear witness—are problems which, in some sense at least, concern *all* believers. Whether or not we accept the terms in which he expresses them—especially perhaps his dichotomy of faith and religion—we must all question the situation of the Christian faith in the world now in formation around us, and the form the Church's presence in that world should take. Since Christianity first began, the 'figure of this world' has been continually changing, and forcing Christians to re-think their position and re-formulate their witness. It is clear that in our time we are seeing the 'disestablishment' of all the Churches. It is a 'disestablishment' to which, in many cases, they are not just submitting, but which they are actually choosing, and which seems to be the pre-condition for a more genuinely spiritual activity. Yet it is equally clear that, if it is true that the Christian faith is rooted, and must always be manifested, in history, then there will be limits to how far it can be 'disestablished'. Bonhoeffer—at least as long as we are careful not to truncate his message—is the first to remind us how complex the problem is, how complex the apparently paradoxical terms that must be reconciled: on the one hand we must not make the Church and the truths of faith simply a 'bit' of the world; and on the other, we must truly bear witness to the faith in this world, and doing so will necessarily mean giving it, at both individual and community level, a certain 'image'.

Even if Christians of different confessions are not yet ready to resolve this vital problem together and in the same way, it is the problem of what concrete form their witness must take, and all their researches are in effect concerned with the same point.

If I am asked myself to say how I would best like to see that research carried out, I should like to suggest the theme of 'sacramentality', particularly as outlined in the early part of the dogmatic constitution, *Lumen Gentium*. How is the Church, how are we as Christians to be effective 'signs' of God, bearing witness to his presence and his work of reconciling all things, without either arrogating his functions to ourselves or putting up any kind of smokescreen in front of them, and yet actually representing them? This is of course a question for every age, but it faces us with fresh urgency in our unbelieving world today.

All the Churches are aware of the work of research they must now do if they are to fulfil their mission faithfully; what help might they not have got from this man, silenced before his time, who would undoubtedly have had so much to say to us still! Yet even what he has left us, though we cannot hope to find in it a solution in the strict sense, does still serve to stimulate us. And the encounter we can still have with Bonhoeffer in his writings seems to me one which should be of first priority for us all.